The FLAGS of
CIVIL WAR SOUTH CAROLINA

The FLAGS of CIVIL WAR SOUTH CAROLINA

By Glenn Dedmondt

PELICAN PUBLISHING COMPANY
GRETNA 2018

First printing, May 2000
Second printing, September 2018

---

*The word "Pelican" and the depiction of a pelican are
trademarks of Pelican Publishing Company, Inc., and are
registered in the U.S. Patent and Trademark Office.*

Illustrations by the author

Library of Congress Cataloging-in-Publication Data

Dedmondt, Glenn.
    The flags of Civil War South Carolina / by Glenn Dedmondt.
        p. cm.
    Includes bibliographical references.
    ISBN 978-1-56554-696-7 (alk. paper)
        1. Flags—South Carolina. 2. South Carolina—History—Civil War, 1861-1865—Flags. 3.
South Carolina—History—Civil War, 1861-1865—Regimental Histories. 4. United
States—History—Civil War, 1861-1865—Flags. 5. United States—History—Civil War,
1861-1865—Regimental histories. I. Title.

CR114.S6 D43 2000
929.9'2'09757—dc2I
                                                                                                00-020694

Printed in the United States of America

Published by Pelican Publishing Company, Inc.
1000 Burmaster Street, Gretna, Louisiana 70053
www.pelicanpub.com

Contents

I. Antebellum & Early War
On Flags and Heroes

1. Sovereignty Flag (Lone star) . . 13
2. Lone Star & Palmetto Flags . . 14
3. Columbia 15
4. Palmetto Guard (John Bird) . . 16
5. Sovereignty Flag (Stanley Bldg.) 18
6. Sovereignty Flag (Chester County) 19

II. Garrison & Post Flags
A Flag is Born

7. Fort Sumter (1st National) 21
8. Patriotic Miniatures 22
9. 1st National Flag (Matanzas) 23
10. Palmetto Fire Company 24
11. Charleston Signal Flag 25
12. Fort Sumter Signal Flag 26
13. 1st National (variant) 27
14. Washington Artillery 28
15. Fort Sumter (2nd National) . . . 29
16. Fort Sumter Battle Flag 30

III. Cavalry Commands
Distinctively South Carolina

17. 3rd Battalion 32
18. 3rd Battalion (Guidons) 33
19. Williamsburg Light Dragoons 34
20. Lone Star Dragoons 36
21. 5th Regiment 1 37
22. 5th Regiment 2 38
23. South Carolina Rangers (Co. D) 39
24. Cadet Rangers 40
25. Independent Mounted Rifles . . 44

IV. Infantry Regiments & Companies

26. 1st Regiment Rifles (Orr's) . . .45
27. 1st (Gregg's) Regiment 1 46
28. 1st (Gregg's) Regiment 2 47

Those Soul-stirring Blue Banners

29. Edisto Rifles (Co. A, 1st [Hagood's] Regt.) 50
30. Richland Rifles (Co. A, 1st [Gregg's] Regt.) 51
31. Pee Dee Rifles (Co. D 52
32. Union Dist. Volunteers (Co. E) 53
33. Monticello Guards (Co. I) 54
34. Saluda Guards 1 (Co. O) 55
35. Saluda Guards 2 (Co. O) 56
36. Hampton Legion 1 57
37. Hampton Legion 2 59
38. Washington Light Infantry (Co. A) 60
39. Claremont Rifles (Co. G) 61
40. German Volunteers (Co. H) . .62
41. S.C. Zouave Volunteers (Co. H2) .63
42. Edgefield Hussars (Co. A) . . .64
43. Beaufort District Troop (Co. C) 65

The Unfolding of the Battle Flag

44. 2nd Regiment 70
45. Palmetto Guards (Co. I) 71
46. 3rd Regiment 73
47. Williams Guards (Co. B) 74
48. Laurens Briars (Co. G) 76
49. 4th Regiment 1 77

50. 4th Regiment 2 79
51. 5th Regiment 81
52. Johnson Riflemen (Co. A) . . .82
53. Pea Ridge Volunteers (Co. B) 83
54. Kings Mountain Guard (Co. F)
. 84
55. Catawba Light Infantry (Co. H)
. 85
56. Palmetto Sharpshooters 1 . . .86
57. Palmetto Sharpshooters 2 . . .87
58. 6th Regiment 88
59. 7th Regiment 1 89
60. 7th Regiment 2 90
61. 7th Battalion 1 91
62. 7th Battalion 2 92
63. Malvern Hill Flag 93
64. 8th Regiment 94
65. 10th Regiment 1 95
66. 10th Regiment 2 96

Those War-torn Flags

67. 11th Regiment 1 99
68. 11th Regiment 2 100
69. 12th Regiment 102
70. 13th Regiment 103
71. Brockman Guards (Co. B) . .104

The Hiding of the Colors

72. 14th Regiment 107
73. Ryan Guards (Co. H)/ McCalla
Rifles (Co. I). 108
74. 15th Regiment 109
75. Lexington Guards 110
76. 16th Regiment 111
77. Sharpsburg Flag 112
78. Hagood's Brigade (name) . . .113
79. Hagood's Brigade (star) 114
80. 21st Regiment 1 115

81. 21st Regiment 2 116
82. 21st Regiment 3 117
83. Wallace's Brigade 118
84. 24th Regiment 119
85. 25th Regiment 1 121
86. 25th Regiment 2 122
87. 26th Regiment 123
88. Charleston Light Infantry . .124
89. 27th Regiment 125

**V. Artillery Regiments &
Companies**

90. Calhoun Light Battery. 126
91. 1st Regiment. 127
92. Inglis Light Artillery. 128
93. 3rd Regiment Heavy 129
94. Beaufort Volunteer Artillery 130
95. Chesterfield Artillery 131
96. Washington Artillery (Hart's)
. 132
97. German Artillery(Bachmann's)
. 133
98. Ferguson's Battery 1 134
99. Ferguson's Battery 2 135
100. Palmetto Artillery. 136
101. Lafayette Artillery. 137
102. Wagner Light Artillery 138
103. Chesnut Light Artillery . . .140
104. Marion Artillery 142
105. Washington Artillery (Walter's)
. 143

VI. Naval Flags

106. Naval Ensign 144
107. Naval Commission Pennant
. 145
108. Naval Jack. 146

This Book is Respectfully Dedicated
to
Sgt. Adam Carpenter,
Color Bearer, 24th Regt., S.C.V.

And his Compatriots,
The Men from South Carolina Who Bore These Colors.
They Were the Heart of the Regiment,
The Soul of the Battle Line,
The Impetus of the Assault,
And the Focal Point of the Enemy's Fire.

On Flags and Heroes

Flags are implements of war that have no violent purpose. They make no demands. They do not destroy, tear down, maim, or kill. Their purpose is to stir the most noble emotions within the human heart, emotions such as *selflessness, bravery, familial love, filial love, duty to God and to home,* and *duty to a cause that supercedes one's own selfish motives.* The effects of a flag seem to reach into the deepest recesses of the human psyche, not the primitive part that demands that we breathe and feed ourselves, but the part that harbors the deepest and most noble motives, feelings that prove that man is truly made in the image of God.

South Carolinians have a great appreciation for flags. The Capitol dome in Columbia is the only dome in the nation displaying three flags. It is common for homeowners to have flagpoles attached to or in front of their houses and for college students to display flags in their dormitory windows. Flags decorate T-shirts, ball caps, and the front bumpers of tens of thousands of our automobiles. In a great many cases, the flag being displayed is the Confederate battle flag with its cross of St. Andrew, or the Crescent and Palmetto tree on a blue (sometimes red) background. Middle school students draw them in their writer's notebooks, college students sew them onto their bookbags, some of the more daring have them tattooed on their arms, and South Carolinians of all walks of life display them on their front lawns for the passing world to see.

And of course, the passing world has responded. South Carolinians have been accused of, among other things, living in the past. The Confederate flags have been under assault from "outsiders" for decades, but each attack has caused South Carolinians to cling tighter to the flags that remind them of a different world, a world in which *bravery, honor, duty,* and *selflessness* were considered worthy virtues. At the time of this writing, there are still some South Carolinians whose *fathers* served in the Confederate army. The Stars and Bars and the Battle Flag with its St. Andrew's cross are truly the flags of their fathers. Other South Carolinians have grandfathers, or great-grandfathers, who served under this flag. Many have researched the service records at the South Carolina State Archives and have discovered one, two, or more ancestors who fought under the Southern Cross. This sense of family, history, and belonging is not isolated to any one part of the state. History is an interwoven part of the mind of South Carolina. South Carolinians are aware that, at a point in history, their state stood alone in its quest for self-government. When challenged by outside powers, their fathers, grandfathers, and great-grandfathers took up arms and marched away under a new flag to defend state sovereignty. The world has recognized the selfless devotion of the Confederate soldier, and their descendants show respect for their ancestors' sacrifices by flying their flag in places of honor.

The dedication of the South Carolina soldier who fought in the Confederate War is part of the historical record. One historian has calculated that South Carolina furnished for the war effort 33 regiments and 2 battalions of infantry, 7 regiments and 1 battalion of cavalry, 1 regiment and 1 battalion of heavy artillery, and 28 batteries of light artillery. South Carolina actually furnished for the service *more* than her "military population" of 55,046. Casualties are hard to reckon; most numbers are only estimates, but a conservative estimate is that 94,000 Confederate soldiers were killed or mortally wounded during the war. Of these approximately 23,000 were South Carolinians. South Carolina lost to the war almost *one-fourth* of her entire male population. The price paid in the quest for South Carolina's independence was staggering.

The survivors came home with nothing to show for their efforts. In some cases their homes had been lost to the savagery of war. Their towns were wrecked. Their economy was in a shambles. After the war, a cruel and debilitating Reconstruction was imposed on the Southern states. For eleven dark years in South Carolina, the surviving veterans were forbidden to express Confederate sympathies, to wear Confederate symbols, or to fly the Confederate flag. Perhaps the severity of South Carolina's punishment for daring to be free helped to cause the uplifting of all things Confederate when the state finally shook off the Reconstruction shackles in 1876. Regimental associations were formed, uniforms were worn, monuments erected, and flags were flown. In 1896, the United Confederate Veterans passed the torch to their sons, a group that grew stronger through the twentieth century and who now dedicate themselves *"to the defense of the Confederate soldier's good name, the guardianship of his history, the emulation of his virtues"* and *"the perpetuation of those principles he loved and which made him glorious."* Through the work of the Sons of Confederate Veterans, the flag of the South Carolina Confederate soldier flies in a place of honor above the Capitol dome. Today, when the middle school student draws the flag in his writer's notebook, or when a local citizen displays the flag from his front porch, or the college student sews the flag on her bookbag, or when a descendant lovingly places the battle flag over his ancestor's grave on Confederate Memorial Day, each one in his own individual way is saying, "Thank you . . . I remember . . . You are not forgotten."

The **FLAGS** of
CIVIL WAR SOUTH CAROLINA

Sovereignty Flag

The oldest symbol of South Carolina, predating even the Palmetto tree, is the crescent. In medieval England, the crescent was an heraldic emblem representing the second son of the family. Perhaps early South Carolinians identified with this "second son" concept, because the symbol is on South Carolina's first flags of the American Revolution. At the battle of Sullivan's Island, on June 28, 1776, a blue flag with silver crescent was the center of heroic action and became the state's battle flag.

When South Carolina seceded from the Union on December 20, 1860, the above flag was raised over the Customs House in Charleston. The red color, symbolic of fighting spirit, was used on other flags at the time but was for the most part rare, the main color of South Carolina's flags being blue. This flag was later used on the blockade runner, *Dixie*.

One of the earliest "Lone Star" flags made its appearance during the Nullification Crisis (1832). In 1860, many Charleston businesses showed their support by flying similar flags. The Customs House flag is on display in the Confederate Museum in Charleston.

Lone Star and Palmetto Flag

This **Lone Star and Palmetto Flag** is 53¾" (hoist) x 105" (fly). It is made of white bunting in three horizontal strips. The flag is of a naval type and may have been captured from a blockade runner.

This flag eventually came into the possession of Assistant Secretary of the Navy Gustav V. Fox, who gave the flag to John Murray Forbes. The flag was subsequently donated to the Massachusetts Commandery of the Military Order of the Loyal Legion of the United States.

U.S. Army Military History Research Center at Carlisle Barracks, Pa.

Little is known of this Lone Star and Palmetto Flag. Its design would link it to merchant shipping. It is made of homespun with a green wool palmetto tree inset in the center and has a blue 5-pointed star sewn in the upper left-hand corner. The hoist is edged with heavy canvas for attaching to the staff. It is 36" (hoist) x 60" (fly).

One story has it being found in the bottom of a chest in California. At one point in its history, it was on display in the Texas State Archives, Austin, Texas. Nothing more is known of its historical associations.

The Charleston Museum, Charleston, S.C.

Columbia

The *U.S.S. Santiago de Cuba* captured the steamer **Columbia** on May 15, 1862, in the vicinity of the Bahamas. This English-made ship was carrying a battery of Armstrong guns, powder, shot, shell, small arms, and other military equipment. Also captured was the above palmetto and star flag, presumably held in its stores from earlier service on another vessel, and to be flown once the *Columbia* had entered a Confederate harbor.

The white bunting field of the *Columbia* flag measures 34½" (hoist) x 46¾" (fly). The white canvas heading is 2¾" wide and has a whipped eyelet at either end. The appliqued palmetto tree is 27¼" high and has a brown trunk that tapers to a point below separately appliqued green fronds. Arranged vertically along the heading side of the flag are three red bunting five-pointed stars measuring 5½" in diameter.

The three stars may date the flag to early January 1861, and would represent South Carolina, Georgia, and Mississippi.

Smithsonian Institution, Washington, D.C.

Palmetto Guard
Pvt. John Bird's Flag

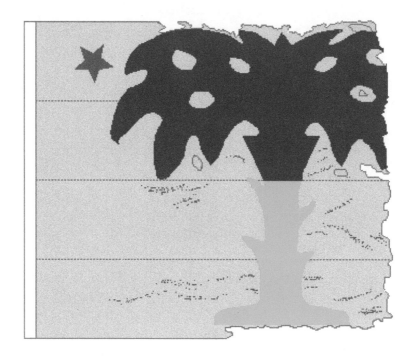

The "Lone Star and Palmetto" flag pictured above created a stir in New York harbor in late November 1860. At that time it was flying from the mast-head of the Palmetto Line brig *John H. Jones*. Reports vary regarding reaction to the flag. One story says that a New York gentleman "politely questioned" Capt. Charles E. Mills about the flag, while other stories say that the ship was "mobbed" by irate citizens. No matter what the reaction of the northern public was, the response of Capt. Mills was clear. The flag would remain in its place of prominence on the ship. It actually was brought down at sometime during the ship's stay in New York, during which time a red star was painted in the top left corner, a star representing the Republic of South Carolina. It was then returned to its position atop the mast.

Captain Mills was given a hero's welcome when he returned to South Carolina. For his obstinate bravery, he was presented a beautiful, gold-headed cane upon which was inscribed, "Presented to Chas. E. Mills, By his Charleston Friends, Dec. 21st, 1860." In return for his involvement in this presentation, John S. Bird, a military goods dealer and member of the Palmetto Guard, was given the flag flown by Mills in New York. Private Bird carried the flag as an unofficial company flag of the Palmetto Guard beginning at that time.

On December 30, 1860, when South Carolina troops occupied the Charleston Arsenal, Pvt. Bird's flag was run up the flagstaff. On January 9, 1861, the unit was transferred to Morris Island and the flag was flown from the old Charleston Lighthouse. On March 11, the Palmetto Guard was ordered to Cummings Point and established camp near Stevens' Iron Battery. Pvt. Bird's flag flew over this camp where the soldiers were retrained as artillerymen.

During the bombardment of Fort Sumter, Bird's flag was being raised on the Iron Battery when the first shot from Sumter was fired and passed within a few feet of the staff.

With Major Anderson's surrender of the fort, Morris Island commander Brig. Gen. James Simons requested the use of Bird's flag for identification to meet "Union States barges" approaching from the island. The flag was then returned to Bird.

The Palmetto Guard was designated by General Beauregard as one of the units to occupy Fort Sumter. They boarded the steamer *Excel* for Sumter, where they were positioned on the granite wharf to prevent civilian sightseers from interfering with the forthcoming surrender ceremony. Upon landing, Private Bird was stationed near the sally port. After being relieved from his post, he secured a pole from the *Excel* and attached the flag. When the last Federal exited the fort and boarded a steamer, Bird raced into the fort, up a stairway, and planted the flag on the left flank parapet, making this flag the first Southern flag to fly over Fort Sumter.

On April 15, the Palmetto Guard was ordered back to Morris Island. In late April, the company was assigned to the 2nd Regiment S.C. Infantry as Company I. From Charleston the regiment went to Virginia, where the flag was carried into battle as the regiment fought at 1st Manassas.

In 1861, Bird was discharged for physical disability and went home with the flag. Bird carried the flag at the 1899 UCV reunion in Charleston. He died in 1906 with the family keeping the flag, until his grandson, John Styles Ashe, donated it to Fort Sumter NM in 1979.

Fort Sumter National Monument, Charleston, S.C.

State Sovereignty Flag
Stanley Building

This 32" (hoist) x 45" (fly) flag was returned to South Carolina in the fall of 1923, over 58 years after its capture. Sergeant Samuel Dodge, a signalman in Sherman's army, was a member of the advance troops entering Columbia, S.C., in February 1865. When he left, he took with him the flag from the Stanley Building. After the war, the flag was kept in a barn on his Illinois farm with other war relics until his death, when it was sent to his brother, Captain J. True Dodge.

The presence of this flag gained publicity in 1921 when it was placed on display in Illinois during the 58th anniversary of the battle of Chickamauga. Mrs. S.D. McKenny, of the Illinois D.A.R., informed the South Carolina delegate of the flag's whereabouts. Mrs. Della Richards Coulter, president of the Wade Hampton Camp, U.D.C., made an appeal to Captain Dodge for the flag's return and in the fall of that year was rewarded for her efforts with a package in the mail containing the above flag.

At the next meeting of the Wade Hampton chapter, a vote was taken and the flag was formally presented to the Confederate Relic Room and Museum.

South Carolina Confederate Relic Room & Museum, Columbia, S.C.

Chester County Sovereignty Flag

Many refer to this design and color pattern as that of the *South Carolina Sovereignty Flag*, having made its appearance during the days of the secession meetings. The blue field was traditional from 1776, as were the crescent and the palmetto. The red cross of St. George reflected the English heritage and Christian faith of South Carolina. The thirteen stars most likely represented the original thirteen colonies who "seceded" from the English union, with the center star representing South Carolina. Considering the heavy religious symbolism of the flag, the parallel representation of Christ and his disciples in the arrangement of stars cannot be discounted.

The design and color pattern of this flag were later adopted in the Army of Tennessee by General Leonidas Polk for use in his Corps, with the St. George's cross reflecting Polk's status as an ordained Episcopal bishop.

Chester County Historical Society Museum, Chester, S.C.

This handmade flag is 28½"(hoist) x 39" (fly). It is one of the few surviving examples of this rare flag in existence.

A Flag is Born

After the repulsed invasion of South Carolina waters on January 9, 1861, six more states joined her in secession from the Union. In February of that year, they formed a coalition of republics patterned after the original pact formed by the Articles of Confederation of 1776. They selected a name, the Confederate States of America, and adopted a flag that harked back to the original flag of the republic. The body of the flag was composed of three horizontal bars, from top to bottom, red/white/red. In the top hoist corner was a blue canton with a circle of seven white stars signifying, as in the Betsy Ross flag, the equality of all states and the dominance of none. It is said that the three horizontal bars were meant to reflect the spiritual nature of the newly formed country and were designed to represent the Trinity of the Christian faith. The Confederate Congress, before the final approval, considered many different, and strikingly unusual, designs. Two men claim to have designed this flag. A Prussian artist, Nicola Marschall, said that he based his design on the Austrian tricolor. His letter of suggestion dated March 2, 1861, seems to back this claim. A second designer, Orren R. Smith, a North Carolinian, said that he designed the flag as a symbol of the Trinity. In 1915, the United Confederate Veterans gave Smith's claim their seal of approval, although in 1931, the Alabama Archives produced a study accepting Marschall's claim. It is possible that both men produced their designs concurrently.

During the life of the Confederacy there were actually three official national flags. This flag is referred to as the *First National.* It is remembered by the nickname, *The Stars and Bars,* and is prominent in South Carolina history as the *Fort Sumter Flag.*

After fighting began between the South and the North, many southern regiments marched off to the front under regimental flags based entirely or mostly on the Confederate First National. Prominent among these are the flags of *Hagood's Brigade,* notably the *11th* and *21st S.C. Regiments.* The star patterns were sometimes different. Some patterns include a state seal in the canton. One South Carolina variant shows the state motto and a semi-circle of stars. Though the Stars and Bars was taken from national use in May 1863 with the adoption of the Stainless Banner, units in the field continued using it. At the surrender of their army, men of Hagood's Brigade tore their 1st National flag into pieces rather than surrender it.

Fort Sumter Garrison Flag

South Carolina seceded from the United States on December 20, 1860. As a result of the Federal invasion of Charleston Harbor on January 9, 1861, six other states severed their ties with the Union. In a convention in Montgomery, Alabama, these seven states formed a new government, a confederacy based on the original government of 1776. They adopted a flag that, with its circle of stars, was also based on the flag of the first government. This flag is remembered as the 1st National Flag of the Confederacy, or the "Stars and Bars."

As peaceful efforts failed to remove the Federal contingency in Fort Sumter, and with word of a second resupply mission coming from the north, a siege of the fort began on April 12, 1861, and ended with the surrender of Union Major Robert Anderson.

Charleston authorities wanted to raise over Fort Sumter the first flag that had flown over the new government in Montgomery. Unable to obtain that flag in time, a rush order was placed with a Charleston ship chandler, J.E. Vincent, for this camp-size (4½ feet by 7 feet) flag to raise over Fort Sumter.

On the morning of April 18, 1861, the batteries around Charleston thundered in salute of this new flag representing a new nation. As the sounds of the firing echoed across the harbor, Captain Samuel Ferguson of South Carolina's state navy raised the Stars and Bars to the top of a 15-foot-high staff lashed to one of the guns of Sumter's eastern rampart, facing Charleston.

Confederate Museum, Charleston, S.C.

Patriotic Miniatures

Even in the early morning hours of April 12, 1861, many citizens of Charleston lay awake in their beds. They knew that the time for a graceful and peaceful evacuation of Fort Sumter was nearing an end. The diarist, Mary Chesnut, remembered:

> *I do not pretend to go to sleep. How can I? If Anderson does not accept terms at four, the orders are, he shall be fired upon. I count four, St. Michael's bells chime out and I begin to hope. At half-past four the heavy booming of a cannon. I sprang out of bed and on my knees prostrate I prayed as I never prayed before.*

> *There was a sound of stir all over the house, pattering of feet in the corridors. All seemed hurrying one way. I put on my double-gown and a shawl and went, too. It was to the housetop. The shells were bursting...The women were wild there on the housetop. Prayers came from the women and imprecations from the men. And then a shell would light up the scene.*

On April 12, 1861, during the firing on Fort Sumter, Mrs. N. Russell Middleton made the small flag pictured above for her son Russell to wave from their house. It is approximately 12" (hoist) x 16" (fly) and is made of cotton.

Confederate Museum, Charleston, S.C.

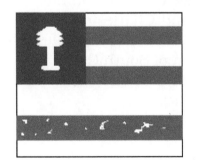

This small (8½" x 10") crudely made banner was found and stolen by Federal soldiers from the home of General Thomas Drayton on Hilton Head Island on November 8, 1861. The Union troops in that area were the 3rd N.H. Volunteers.

This flag was probably sewn between February and April of 1861, with the stripes representing the first seven states of the Confederacy.

South Carolina State Museum, Columbia, S.C.

1st National Flag
Matanzas, Cuba/Steamer *Gordon*

The *Gordon* was a 177' side-wheeler built in New York in 1851. She was first owned by a stock company that used her as a privateer. The *Gordon* was one of only two privateers that ran the blockade to undertake their raids. By the end of August 1861 they both had returned to port, their privateering days ended by Union vigilance. In August of 1861, she was purchased by John Fraser and Company and renamed the *Theodora.* She was owned by the Florida Steam Packet Company and based in Charleston, South Carolina. During her career as a blockade-runner, she successfully ran the Union blockade six times.

While the *Gordon/Theodora* was in Cuba, a group of ladies of Matanzas presented this beautiful silk flag to the captain.

The flag is 55" (hoist) x 126" (fly) and displays eleven metallic yarn stars on a blue silk canton. Red and gold, the Spanish national colors, were likely used to demonstrate the close relationship existing between the Confederacy and the Spanish people of Cuba.

Confederate Museum, Charleston, S.C.

Palmetto Fire Company

When South Carolina seceded from the Union, the militia was the new republic's first and only line of defense. The largest and most organized body of militia was the Fourth Brigade of Charleston, under General James Simons. The brigade was composed of the 1st Regiment of Rifles, the 17th Regiment, the 1st Artillery Regiment, four light batteries, three companies of cavalry, and a Volunteer Corps of fire departments. These fire companies did faithful and efficient duty throughout the war, both as firemen and as soldiers. They drilled regularly and performed guard duty. This flag was passed down from the Volunteer Fire Department through Thomas Miller to its current location at the Washington Light Infantry.

This small 1st National Flag is 30" (hoist) x 36" (fly). The canton is 19" (vertical) x 17" (horizontal). The seven stars are 3" point to point. The flag is bordered on three sides with 1½" gold fringe.

It is made of silk. Its blue canton retains its color, while the two red bars have faded nearly white. The flag is in very fragile condition.

Washington Light Infantry, Charleston, S.C.

Charleston Signal Flag

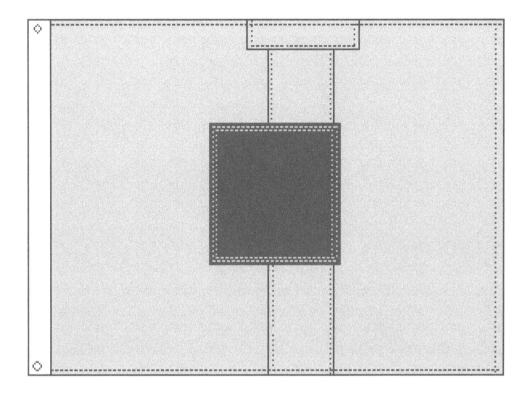

This **signal flag** is 26" (hoist) x 34" (fly), with a 2½" canvas heading with two whipped eyelets. The red center is 10½" (vertical) x 10" (horizontal). The body is made of assorted pieces of white muslin.

Signal flags such as this were used on a single staff and waved in a wig-wag pattern. If the flag was waved to one side of the signalman, it would represent a one. The other side was a two. Messages could be sent quickly around the harbor using a code similar to Morse code, only with patterns of numbers representing each letter. The obvious drawback would be that Union blockaders could read the messages through their telescopes. The messages were therefore encrypted with a code that changed on a regular basis.

According to Signalman A.L. Doty, Jr., this signal flag "was used at nearly every station around Charleston during the Civil War." It was presented to the Washington Light Infantry by Doty on March 24, 1879.

Washington Light Infantry, Charleston, S.C.

Fort Sumter Signal Flag

This signal flag is 36" x 36" and is made of four strips of red cotton sewn horizontally. The white square in the center is 8¼" high x 8½" wide. It was used at Fort Sumter and is accompanied by the following letter, written from Augusta, Ga., May 24, 1920.

Dear Miss Washington,

I wish to turn over to the Charleston Chapter, U.D.C., this flag. I was on duty in Fort Sumter at the surrender and in the Signal Corps. The flag was used as the Signal Flag. I had been on duty there and in St. Michael's steeple and was at the Fort at the windup. By order of Capt. Thomas Huguenin, who was in command, I was detailed to count out the garrison at the sally port when we embarked on leaving the Fort. I remember counting and found one short and calling to report to Capt. Huguenin he could not be found. I went through the gallery and found him in his quarters and told him the boat was waiting on him and he said he "had rather die in Fort Sumter than live outside it." He was urged to go aboard and the boat steamed away and the garrison debarked at Strawberry Ferry, as I remember the name. After reaching Cheraw, the Signal Corps was disbanded and I went to my old regiment, the 1st Georgia, consolidated and surrendered at Greensboro, N.C. It is a trifling thing in the eyes of any but a patriotic boy who gave 4 of the best years of his life, from 16 to 20, to his country, is today unreconstructed, vowed when paroled I would never take the oath and never have, tho am loyal now to Uncle Sam.

Very truly yours,

Jas. L. Fleming

Confederate Museum, Charleston, S.C.

1ˢᵗ National (variant)

South Carolina

This variation of the Confederate 1ˢᵗ National Flag bears the motto of South Carolina, *animis opibusque parati* (prepared in mind and resources), or as in the translation on the flag of the Williams Guards, *Always Ready.*

South Carolina Confederate Relic Room & Museum, Columbia, S.C.

On February 4, 1998, actor and historian Tom Berenger presented this flag to the state of South Carolina. Although the newspaper text said "The flag is believed to have flown over Charleston, S.C. at the start of the Civil War," the presence of eleven stars would indicate a production date later than May 20, 1861, the secession date of the last state to join the Confederacy.

Washington Artillery
(Resewn from Federal Flag)

This flag was originally the Federal flag presented to the **Washington Artillery** upon its organization in 1844 by ladies of Charleston. When South Carolina seceded, the flag was altered to its present form and hoisted on a staff at the rear of the Washington Artillery gun shed. It is thought to be the first "Stars and Bars" ever hoisted. When the company left for active service, the flag was put in a chest in the armory. It was later placed in the care of a lady (later Mrs. Richard Morris) who kept it through the war. After the evacuation of Charleston, she sewed it into her pillow and slept on it every night.

After the war, the Battery was reorganized and the flag was returned to it. Later, when the Battery was dissolved, the flag was presented by Mrs. Morris to the Confederate Museum.

This flag is 36" (hoist) x 90" (fly). All but twelve of the original stars are covered in blue. The flag was attached to its staff with four pairs of ribbon-type ties. Written on the hoist are the numbers and letters "17-F" and "NYV" or "NYU."

Confederate Museum, Charleston, S.C.

Fort Sumter Garrison Flag

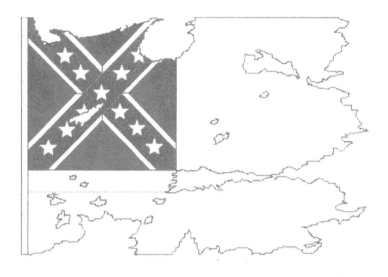

The defense of Fort Sumter must be remembered as one of the most gallant efforts in the history of war. Throughout the war, the fort was the focal point of Union attacks and suffered from many extended bombardments.

The third great bombardment began on July 7, 1864. On the first day of the siege, the flagstaff was shot down three times and the flag torn to pieces. Each time it was replaced. The chief engineer at Sumter, Capt. John Johnson, ordered 1000 bags of sand to be delivered each night.

At this time the fort was commanded by Capt. John C. Mitchel. After lunch on July 20 and prior to writing his daily report, he climbed to the western angle of the gorge to observe the movements of the blockading squadron. While he was at the sandbagged sentry station, a mortar shell burst overhead and a shell fragment fell from about eighty feet, striking him on the hip. The wound proved serious. He was carried below, bleeding profusely, and died four hours later. Capt. Thomas Huguenin then took command of the fort.

The third bombardment ended on September 8, 1864. The Union artillery had fired at the fort 14,666 rounds, many weighing 200-300 pounds each, and yet the fort stood, its gunners returning fire from behind sandbags and piles of bricks.

The 2nd National Flag shown above was "flown at Ft. Sumter when Capt. John C. Mitchell (sic) was killed there." It shows numerous signs of repair, an almost "puzzle like construction", and displays vividly the effects of one of Sumter's most terrible bombardments. The hoist is 77". The fly as it exists in its tattered state is 80".

The Charleston Museum, Charleston, S.C.

Fort Sumter Battle Flag

After the death of Captain John C. Mitchel on July 20, 1864, Captain Thomas Huguenin assumed command of Fort Sumter. This battle flag flew over Fort Sumter from July 30, 1864 until the fort was evacuated on February 19, 1865.

It is 46" (hoist) x 46" (fly), and has a 2" border on three sides with a 2" canvas heading on the hoist. The St. Andrew's cross is made of 8" blue bars bordered with 1" fimbriation. The stars are 4" in diameter.

W. George Gibbs presented this flag to the Washington Light Infantry on July 19, 1878.

Washington Light Infantry, Charleston, S.C.

Distinctively South Carolina

While South Carolina volunteers were arriving in Virginia and being issued the now familiar Army of Northern Virginia battle flag, a distinctly different type of banner was evolving in the Charleston area. In March of 1862, the editor of the *Charleston Mercury* proposed once again his design for a solution to the 1st National look-alike problem. He suggested a two-colored, four-paneled flag with a color separation being along diagonal lines drawn from corner to corner.

It was evidently about this time that several units in the Charleston area adopted the Mercury flag. Surviving examples would suggest that a combination of red and white designated Infantry and Cavalry, while the combination of blue and white was used by Artillery. The flag of the **Charleston Light Infantry** is of this *Mercury* pattern. Its top and bottom quarter panels are red, the left and right ones being white. Centered on the obverse is a large blue shield bordered in gold. Written in gold on the shield are C.L.I. and SECESSIONVILLE. Other surviving examples are those of the 3rd **Battalion S.C. Cavalry** and the **1st Regiment S.C. Artillery.**

A second flag, individual to South Carolina, saw service in conjunction with the *Mercury* flag. The individual companies of artillery and cavalry often served as independent units and were detached accordingly. While infantry companies were forbidden the use of flags, their use was necessary for artillery and cavalry, so the individual companies of horsemen and cannoneers carried a black and garnet (a color combination still familiar to Gamecock fans) swallowtail guidon.

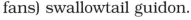

These company flags were horizontal bicolors, the top half being garnet, the bottom half black. Company designators were sewn-on letters and numerals in white (on garnet) and red (on black). The companies of the 3rd (Palmetto) Battalion Light Artillery also used the garnet/black guidons. This would suggest that the Battalion flag might have been of the *Mercury* type, although no such flag has survived.

3rd Battalion Cavalry
South Carolina Volunteers

The 3rd Battalion S.C. Cavalry was organized on May 30, 1862, with seven companies. On July 19, 1862, it was increased to a regiment and redesignated the 3rd Cavalry Regiment, South Carolina Volunteers. This flag was likely replaced by a Charleston Depot battle flag at this time. The regiment served in the Department of South Carolina, Georgia, and Florida.

The flag of the 3rd Battalion S.C. Cavalry is 28" (hoist) x 30" (fly). The background of this flag is composed of red and white quarter panels sewn together and centered with a 9½" blue cloth circle with handpainted patterns in gold. The "3" is 1⅞" tall. The word BATTALION is 7⅜" long and is made up of 1⅝" tall gold letters. The method of pole attachment is a 2" wide red sleeve.

South Carolina Confederate Relic Room & Museum, Columbia, S.C.

This flag was saved on the night of April 2, 1865, during the evacuation of Richmond, Virginia, by Dr. T.A. LaFar and was presented by him to the state of South Carolina.

Company Guidons

3rd Battalion, South Carolina Volunteer Cavalry

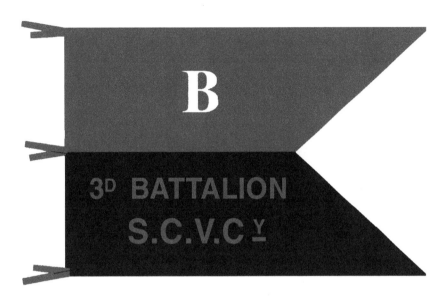

Company B, 3rd Battalion South Carolina Volunteer Cavalry was also known as the Colleton Rangers. They were organized on March 26, 1862 and were first stationed at Jacksonborough, S.C., where they remained until the early winter, when they were deployed to Pocotaligo. They served in the defenses of the South Carolina coast, were transferred to Riceborough, Ga., then to Camp Rogers, Ga., in the spring of 1864. By summer they were back at Pocotaligo. They finished the year at Coosawhatchie.

The company guidon is of a design used only in South Carolina. It is 27" (hoist) x 41" (fly). The letters and numerals are sewn on individually.

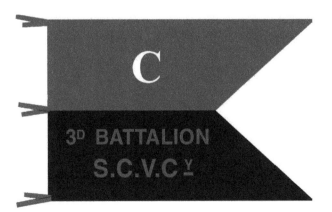

Company C, also known as *Beaufort District Troop,* was organized under Captain John Howard, on March 27, 1862, and was originally stationed at Grahamville, S.C. They saw action at Pinckney Island, August 21, 1862, and at Honey Hill, November 30, 1864.

The guidons of the 3rd Battalion Cavalry were readable on both the obverse and the reverse.

Company D, 3rd Battalion South Carolina Volunteer Cavalry, also known as the Barnwell Dragoons, was organized on March 28, 1862, and was originally stationed at Camp Barnwell. They summered at Grahamville, and spent the fall in camp near Bee's Creek. Other stations were Camp Fripp, Bluffton, and Coosawhatchie. They were engaged at the battle of Honey Hill and skirmished with the enemy during the Union retreat.

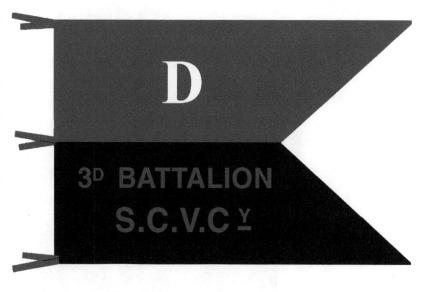

3rd Battalion South Carolina Cavalry/3rd Regiment

Company A:	*Marion Men of Combahee*
Company B:	*Colleton Rangers*
Company C:	*Beaufort District Troop*
Company D:	*Barnwell Dragoons*
Company E:	*Calhoun Mounted Men*
Company F:	*St. Peter's Guards*
Company G:	*German Hussars*
Company H:	*Ashley Dragoons or Rangers*
Company I:	*Rebel Troop*
Company K:	*Savannah River Guards*

Also a section of Horse Artillery under 1st Lt. Richard Johnson and 2nd Lt. Wm. N. Heyward.

The guidons of Companies B, C, and D are at the South Carolina Confederate Relic Room & Museum, Columbia, S.C.

Williamsburg Light Dragoons

Company B, 12th Cavalry Battalion, South Carolina Volunteers

Company I, 4th Cavalry Regiment, South Carolina Volunteers

The 12th Battalion, South Carolina Cavalry, was organized with four companies in the spring of 1862 under Major William P. Emanuel. The **Williamsburg Light Dragoons** formed Company B of the 12th Battalion. In December of that year the battalion was consolidated with the 10th Cavalry Battalion and designated the 4th Cavalry Regiment.

After reorganization, the *Dragoons* were redesignated Company I, 4th South Carolina Cavalry. John Watson was elected captain. Later captains were George P. Nelson and S.J. Snowden. On May 4, 1863, they engaged the enemy at Murray's Inlet, S.C.

During the winter of 1863, Company I was at Battery White. In the spring they moved camp to McPhersonville, where they spent the summer. In November, they took part in the Pocotaligo campaign. In September 1864, they were at Camp Butler.

This flag of the Williamsburg Light Dragoons is 21¾" (hoist) x 32" (fly) and is made of white linen with blue silk patterns sewn on. Both sides of the flag are readable.

South Carolina State Museum, Columbia, S.C.

Lone Star Dragoons
South Carolina Volunteers

The flag of the **Lone Star Dragoons** is 20½" (hoist) x 26¼" (fly) and is made of blue silk. On the obverse is an embroidered gold palmetto tree. Centered on the reverse is the date "1861." Arched above the date in block, all capital Roman uncial letters are the words LONE STAR. In a reverse arch below the date is the word DRAGOONS.

There is thick gold fringe, 4⅞" wide, on three sides. There were silk ties on the hoist side for attaching the flag to the staff. Two ties remain.

The flag is in poor condition, with the silk stained and shredding.

The flag of the *Lone Star Dragoons* was formerly owned by the *Charleston Light Dragoons*, which would establish ties to the *4ᵗʰ S.C. Cavalry Regiment*.

The flag was presented to the Charleston Museum on February 16, 1934, by the American Legion Post No. 10.

Charleston Museum, Charleston, S.C.

5th Regiment Cavalry
South Carolina Volunteers

This Charleston depot flag was presented to the **5th Regiment, S.C. Cavalry** while they served on the South Carolina coast. The regiment was ordered to Virginia in March, 1864. It served with General M.C. Butler's Brigade, then was transferred to Logan's Brigade and fought in the defense of the Carolinas against Sherman.

This flag was captured at the battle of Trevilian Station, Virginia, by the 9th New York Cavalry.

From the turn of the century, it was on display at the U.S. Military Academy at West Point, N.Y. In 1989, a member of the Sons of Confederate Veterans saw the flag on display and spoke to Col. Robert Brown, who at that time was commander of the S.C. Division, S.C.V. Commander Brown, whose ancestor was in the 5th S.C. Cavalry, began a letter-writing campaign petitioning that the flag be returned to South Carolina. He was aided in his quest by S.C. National Guard General T.E. Marchant. The flag was turned over to General Marchant in March of 1990 by the New York National Guard in Washington, D.C.

South Carolina Confederate Relic Room & Museum, Columbia, S.C.

On April 9, 1990, the flag was officially presented to the State of South Carolina at the Confederate Relic Room in Columbia. General Marchant presented the flag to Commander Brown, who in turn presented the flag, on behalf of the S.C. Division, S.C.V., to Mr. John Martin, director of the Confederate Relic Room and Museum.

5th Regiment Cavalry
South Carolina Volunteers

This 56½" (hoist) x 56½" (fly) battle flag of the **5th Regiment, S.C. Cavalry** is an Army of Northern Virginia pattern, 3rd bunting issue, from the Richmond clothing depot. There were many variants of the 3rd issue group of flags. Museum papers refer to this flag as being of a "6th overall issue—Spring 1864." Due to shortages at home, these flags were produced using materials brought in by blockade runner.

It is made of red, blue, and white wool with white cotton trim. The blue St. Andrew's cross is sewn onto the red field and outlined with white cotton fimbriation. Thirteen white cotton stars are sewn on the blue cross and are evenly spaced, giving the flag the typical 3rd issue "balanced" look. Three outside edges of the flag have a 2" wool border. The hoist edge is bound with a 2¼" white cotton band for attaching the flag to the staff.

Museum remarks include "Poor condition, many holes and fragile." A note attached to the flag reads: *Battle flag/5th So. Ca. Cavalry/Butler's Brigade/ A.N.V./1864-1865/Entrusted to the/custody of the/Charleston Light Dragoons/ by/Zimmerman Davis/Col. 5th S.C. Cav.*

This flag was donated to the Charleston Museum by the Charleston Light Dragoons on July 21, 1966.

The Charleston Museum, Charleston, S.C.

South Carolina Rangers

Company D, 5th Regiment Cavalry, S.C. Volunteers

The **South Carolina Rangers** were organized first on November 6, 1860, as an independent cavalry company under Captain R.J. Jeffords. On April 15, 1862, the company was enlisted as Company A, 17th S.C. Volunteer Cavalry Battalion. From this time until the end of the war they served under Captain Davis Zimmerman. On January 18, 1863, the company was reorganized as Company D, 5th S.C. Regiment Cavalry.

The company flag shown above is 28" (hoist) x 31¼" (fly). It is bordered on three sides with 1½" gold metallic fringe. The obverse of the flag has a field of white silk with a hand-painted figure of a soldier on horseback in a circular seal. Arching above the figure is the name of the company. In a reverse arch below is the Latin word SPECTEMURAGENDO.

The reverse of the flag is a field of blue silk with a circle of eleven gold stars. Inside the circle is written in gold, block letters SO. CA./RANGERS/APRIL 13/1861.

The flag is in very poor condition. The silk is cracked in many places and the paint has flaked off.

The Charleston Museum, Charleston, S.C.

Cadet Rangers

Co. F, 16th Bn. S.C. Partisan Rangers;
6th S.C. Cavalry

"Till Victory or Death the struggle shall end"

In June 1862, thirty-six cadets from the S.C. Military Academy resigned and organized themselves into a cavalry company. Criticized by academy administrators, they were praised by Governor Pickens. The **Cadet Rangers** became Company F of Colonel Hugh Aiken's 16th Battalion, South Carolina Partisan Rangers. Later, increased in strength, the unit was redesignated 6th S.C. Cavalry.

Their strikingly beautiful banner was sewn by Misses Annie Brewster, Carrie Desel, and Carrie Waties, and presented to the Rangers on February 18, 1863. Escorted by Lt. Alfred Aldrich, the three young ladies arrived at the parade ground where the company was formed. Lieutenant Aldrich, at the request of the donors, presented the flag to Captain Moses Benbow Humphrey. The young captain clasped it and addressed the assemblage, recounting the events that surrounded the formation of the company. Then, looking at the young ladies from whose hands the banner was born, he charged:

> *"And now that our course has been approved by the great, and has won the smiles of the fair, our duty is still to go forward. For when woman points onward what coward will stand and see shame and dishonor descend on his land?"*

Humphrey closed his remarks, exhorting his subordinates:

"While we who have been less fortunate are equally determined to emulate your virtues, that when we again sue at beauty's altar we may hope to gain a reward. It is with the confidence that each of you will do your duty that I receive this banner in behalf of the Cadet Rangers, and that I tell the fair donors to rest assured that,

One stain of dishonor they never shall see
On the folds of that banner we swear to defend,
Till victory or death the struggle shall end."

Humphrey then handed the banner over to Corporal Gabriel M. Hodges, the company's first color bearer, bidding him:

"And before high heaven, and in the presence of Heaven's God, I charge you never to allow its sacred folds to trail in the dust.

If you fall, sir, with your dying grasp preserve that banner still erect, and let it float proudly to heaven's breeze in the very face of the foe."

In March 1864, the 6th S.C. Cavalry was ordered to Virginia, along with the 4th and 5th Cavalry, to be part of Brigadier General Matthew C. Butler's brigade.

The Rangers were engaged at the battle of Trevilian Station, Virginia. At a crucial juncture at Louisa Courthouse, on June 11, General Wade Hampton personally led the Cadets. This action saved a Confederate battery from capture.

They were called back to South Carolina in February 1865, and fought with Butler's Cavalry on the withdrawal into North Carolina. On March 9, 1865, the 6th Cavalry assisted in the capture of Union Gen. Kilpatrick's rear guard and a stand of colors. On the following day, charging a Union gun position, Captain Humphrey was badly wounded. In a hospital in Charlotte, N.C., he learned of Johnston's surrender on April 26, 1865. He died four days later.

This flag did not survive the war.

(Reverse side)

The Cadet Rangers
at Trevilian Station

In early June, 1864, Union General Philip Sheridan led a force of 6,000 Federal cavalry into Virginia with the goal of destroying a vital section of the Virginia Central Railroad. He felt that the death of General J.E.B. Stuart the previous month left the Cavalry of the Army of Northern Virginia vulnerable and used this opportunity to strike a blow in the heart of Virginia. But on the morning of the 11th of June, Sheridan was intercepted by the Cavalry Corps of the Army of Northern Virginia under its new leader, General Wade Hampton.

Hampton was a celebrity in South Carolina. At his own expense he had personally outfitted a legion of troops, infantry, cavalry, and artillery, a legion that served nobly throughout the war. He was a member of one of South Carolina's oldest families and descended from Revolutionary War patriots. He was wounded at 1st Manassas, Seven Pines, and Gettysburg, and was promoted to General in August 1863.

When Sheridan and Hampton met at Trevilian Station, a fierce battle erupted in dense woods, forcing the cavalrymen to fight at times on foot. In the heat of the fight, however, Hampton seized the opportunity to mount a charge against the Federals in a dusty clearing near the railroad.

"Charge them, my brave boys, charge them!" he ordered, and then personally led the attack atop Butler, his big bay horse. Around him, the troops in gray and butternut surged forward through a haze of smoke and dust, and in

the forefront of the charge was a force of newly-arrived South Carolinians that included The Citadel's **Cadet Rangers.** As was his way, Hampton led with his saber then, in hand-to-hand combat, switched to his revolver. Saddles emptied on both sides. Hampton single-handedly took down three adversaries.

The battle shifted to other parts of the field and continued the next day. It was finally decided when a bold Confederate counterattack shattered the Federal line. On the 13th, Sheridan and his troops retreated with their mission foiled and a lesson learned that the Cavalry Corps of the Army of Northern Virginia was in capable hands.

Independent Mounted Rifles/
James Mounted Riflemen

Company A of this squadron was initially attached to the 6th Battalion, South Carolina Volunteer Infantry, but later became Company D, 4th Regiment South Carolina Volunteer Cavalry; Company B of this squadron later became Company E, 5th South Carolina Volunteer Cavalry.

This flag is 68" (hoist) x 86" (fly). The motto "INDEPENDENT." is painted in black block letters, 5" high (and 75" long overall) below the palmetto tree on both obverse and reverse so as to read correctly on both sides. The field is white cotton/flannel of double thickness on the bottom 11" panel. The palmetto tree is green, 49" high overall, with a 3½"-wide trunk and a 23"-wide base. There are ten dark blue five-pointed stars, nine grouped around the tree, each 8" inches in diameter, and one 21"- to 22½"-diameter star on the tree. All are painted. There is a 1"-wide border along the top of the flag, made of linen.

South Carolina State Museum, Columbia, South Carolina

1st (Orr's) Regiment of Rifles
South Carolina Volunteers

In the spring of 1861, James L. Orr of South Carolina was authorized to raise a regiment of infantry for the service of the Confederate States. The regiment of ten companies remained in training at Sandy Springs, Anderson District, S.C., until it was sent to Sullivan's Island on the coast. Orr's Regiment stayed there until April 1862. Colonel Orr resigned in December 1861 due to his election to the Confederate Senate, and was succeeded by Colonel J. Foster Marshall.

In April 1862, the regiment was ordered to Richmond, where it was assigned to J.R. Anderson's Brigade. Later it was attached to Joseph Kershaw's Brigade and remained there until Lee's surrender at Appomattox.

The flag of the **1st (Orr's) Regiment of Rifles** is 30" (hoist) x 49½" (fly) and has a blue sleeve for mounting. The crescent is 8" point to point and is of white cotton sewn to the blue silk. The Roman uncial letters of the arch are 1⅜" high and are painted in gold and are shaded lower and right in red. The letters and numbers in the date on either side of the palmetto are also Roman uncial, gold painted with red shading lower and right, and are 1¼" high. The total width of the lower lettered phrase is 17".

The stylized palmetto tree reflects a symbolism often apparent on flags of South Carolina. With its eleven fronds, it is a reminder that from the roots of South Carolina's secession came a Confederation of eleven sovereign states. The tree, white cotton, sewn to the blue silk, is 23" tall and at its widest point is 13½". The base is 5¼" wide. The reverse is a 1st National flag of standard proportions with a circle of eleven stars.

South Carolina Confederate Relic Room & Museum, Columbia, S.C.

1st (Gregg's) Regiment Infantry
South Carolina Volunteers

This flag of Gen. Maxcy Gregg's (later Gen. Samuel McGowan's) **1st S.C. Infantry** has a noble and heroic history. It is possibly the first regimental colors unfurled in Virginia (SHSH,XXV,234). In a bloody charge at the Battle of Gaine's Mill on June 27, 1862, these colors changed hands five times, the bearers all teenagers. The flag was borne into battle first by Color Sergeant James "Jimmy" Taylor (16) who was shot three times, with the third wound proving fatal. Corporal Shubrick Hayne (18) picked up the colors and was shot almost immediately. Private Alfred Pinckney retrieved the colors and the charge continued until he fell mortally wounded. Private Gadsden Holmes sprang forward to raise the colors and was shot seven times before he reached it. Private Dominick Spellman, however, saved the flag, and carried it victoriously as the enemy retreated before the Southern charge.

For his bravery, Pvt. Spellman was promoted to Regimental Color Sergeant. He carried this flag until he was shot at Manassas. At Gettysburg, Color Sergeant Larkin was shot through the body as he was crossing the stone wall with the colors.

After Gettysburg, the flag was placed on display in the S.C. State House.

The flag was made by Hayden & Whilden, dealers in military goods at 250 King Street. It was made of blue silk with white embroidery done by Mrs. Philip Schuckman. On the left of the wreath are magnolia leaves and berries. On the right are oak leaves and acorns. The flag is 69" (hoist) x 64" (fly), with its fly end badly tattered.

South Carolina Confederate Relic Room & Museum, Columbia, S.C.

1ˢᵗ Regiment Infantry
South Carolina Volunteers

A second flag was made for the **1ˢᵗ South Carolina Infantry** during October 1861. The *Charleston Mercury of Roman* October 30, 1861, described it as being displayed in the storefront of Hayden & Whilden.

On one side, beautifully embroidered upon a white ground, stands a Palmetto, emblem of the State, with a Crescent in the upper flagstaff corner. Below is the name of the regiment. On the reverse, upon a green ground, is a large white wreath, half oak, half laurel, admirably worked. And in the centre, the words PRO PATRIA—CAMPAIGN 1861. The flag is surrounded by a green fringe, and is of a very proper size, not too heavy for use.

According to the article this flag was to be presented to the First Regiment, "now at Suffolk, Virginia." It is not known, however, if this flag was indeed presented or even used by the regiment.

It measures 35" (hoist) x 44" (fly). The crescent and palmetto are fully embroidered in natural colors. The motto on the reverse is Pro Patria *(For the Homeland)* in an arch above COMPʸ over 1861, all embroidered in gold with brown borders. Three sides are bordered by 2⅜" dark green silk cord fringe. The hoist has a 2¼" sleeve.

South Carolina Confederate Relic Room

Those Soul-stirring Blue Banners

From the beginning of the republic, national defense was held in the hands of local militia companies; small detachments of "minute men" ready to serve at a moment's notice. Throughout South Carolina, companies of a hundred men each formed and enlisted for the service of the state. A few of these companies could trace their history to the first American Revolution. Many others were formed during the Nullification Crisis of the 1830s. Most of these companies were formed as a result of the secession movement. The flags of these units were individual in character and each bore one or more slogans that spoke of truth, loyalty, bravery, and determination. These blue banners signaled the formation of South Carolina's first line of defense.

The foundation of most of these company flags was a blue background, usually silk, with a circular seal portraying a palmetto tree. The selection of the palmetto was inevitable. The heroic action at Sullivan's Island in 1776 forever linked South Carolina with the resilient scrub tree that populated her coastline. In addition to the seal, either on the obverse or reverse, would be a slogan.

These blue flags were for the most part shortlived, but in their brief tenure they spoke volumes regarding the mission and goal of the South Carolina volunteers over whom they waved. In Jalapa, S.C., the **Williams Guards** received a flag with the slogan ALWAYS READY, then a second with the petition, GOD GUIDE US. In Yorkville, the **Catawba Light Infantry** marched away under the slogan OUR RIGHTS WE DEFEND. In York county, the flag of the **Kings Mountain Guards** states, LIKE OUR ANCESTORS WE WILL BE FREE. The **Pee Dee Rifles** served throughout the war under the slogan, UNDER THIS

STANDARD WE WILL CONQUER. In Unionville, the **Union District Volunteers** enlisted under the slogan, OUR RIGHTS AGAINST A WORLD IN ARMS.

When these companies were absorbed into Confederate service, their blue banners were folded and stored. Each company found itself part of a regiment that was part of a brigade or division which was part of a corps, and realized that company flags were not only impractical, they were forbidden. Like the men of the Williams Guard, the men "found that the Company had no use for the flags." So these beautiful, gold-fringed, hand-painted works of art went into storage trunks. Due to their short field lives, these flags have survived in relatively good condition and can be seen in museums around the state.

These blue banners may have had short tenure, but they had done their job. They had stirred the heart, given the young volunteers a sense of focus, and instilled upon their minds the causes for which they fought. But being of "no use," they were stored and forgotten—that is until 1865, when suddenly the relics of the cause became precious to the memory of those who survived. The blue silk treasures were sought out and cared for by the survivors as sacred relics and held in reverential awe at UCV reunions. Finally, when the aged veterans realized that the river was near, their treasures were committed in trust to the safekeeping of the state for which so many laid down their lives.

The 1st South Carolina Volunteers was the first regiment to come to the defense of the Republic of South Carolina. They began arriving in Charleston as early as January 3, 1861. On the 28th of that month they were sufficiently trained to be inspected by Governor Francis W. Pickens, accompanied by his wife and daughter. The Richland Rifles (Co. A) from Columbia and the Rhett Guard (Co. L) from Newberry are shown in formation with their company banners.

Edisto Rifles

Company A, 1st (Hagood's) Regiment, S.C.V.

The **Edisto Rifles** were formed in Orangeburg, S.C., in 1851. They elected as their captain John J. Salley. Subsequent commanders were John V. Glover and William L. Ehmay. After South Carolina's secession, the rifles volunteered for service and were reorganized for active duty on January 22, 1861. Thomas J. Glover was elected captain.

When the 1st (Hagood's) Regiment was formed, the *Edisto Rifles* became Company A of that regiment and provided the regiment with its first lieutenant colonel, Thomas J. Glover.

In his book, *Edisto Rifles*, William V. Izlar remembered the acquisition of the company colors. His description, written in 1914, though fascinating for its historic significance, has a few errors as to the flag's appearance.

> *"The Edisto Rifles, before leaving Orangeburg for Charleston to join in the attack on Fort Sumter, had been presented with a company flag by Miss Adella Felder, a sister of First Lieutenant John H. Felder of the company, the presentation ceremonies taking place in front of the court house. The material of this flag was blue bunting . . . on one side was a white silk palmetto tree and white silk crescent . . . Beneath the palmetto tree was a . . . scroll on which was the latin motto, 'In hoc signo vinces' . . . The staff was ornamented with a silver star at the top. The flag was delivered to Wm. W. Legare, who was then the color bearer of the company. B.W. Izlar, John C. Pike, and L. Hayne Culler were the color guard."* [errors omitted]

South Carolina Confederate Relic Room & Museum, Columbia, S.C.

Richland Rifles

Co. A, 1st Regiment Infantry, South Carolina Volunteers

The **Richland Volunteer Rifle Company** was formed in Columbia, South Carolina, on August 8, 1813. It was one of the first two companies to answer the call for volunteers and arrived in Charleston on January 3, 1861. The flag shown above was probably presented to the company after their arrival in Charleston.

The flag is 47" (hoist) x 54" (fly). It is made of medium blue silk with a 2½" white silk border on all four sides. It is edged on three sides with a yellow twisted cotton fringe. Centered on the reverse is a naturally colored brocade palmetto tree with two small elliptical shields at its base. Embroidered on the left shield is the date JULY 4 surrounded by the motto ANIMIS OPIBUSQUE PARATI. The shield on the right bears the date MARCH 26 and the motto DUM SPIRO SPERO SPES, all letters in gold. To either side of the tree are the names of the company's various commanders. The obverse bears an embroidered rattlesnake ready to strike. Below is the motto SEMPER PARATI, while above is the phrase NOLI ME TANGERE, both embroidered in gold uncial letters. The names of other commanders, MICKLE, DESAUSSURE, RADCLIFFE, MILLER, and McMAHON are on the obverse.

South Carolina Confederate Relic Room & Museum, Columbia, S.C.

Pee Dee Rifles/Pee Dee Artillery
Co. D, 1st Regiment Infantry/
Co. C, 18th Battalion, S.C. Artillery

The **Pee Dee Rifles** were organized by members of the disbanded *Darlington Guards* and left South Carolina on August 15, 1861. While the 1st Regiment was stationed at Suffolk during the winter of 1862, the company was converted to field artillery and redesignated the **Pee Dee Artillery.** As a part of Pegram's artillery battalion, Army of Northern Virginia, they participated in battles at Spottsylvania, Hanover Junction, and Cold Harbor. They returned to South Carolina in June, 1864, and became Co. C., 18th Bn., S.C. Artillery (Manigault's), also known as the S.C. Siege Train.

While the company was at Suffolk during the fall of 1861, Colonel Gregg presented the Pee Dee Rifles with a flag made by Miss Louisa McIntosh and "other ladies of Society Hill." With a 37" hoist and a 40" fly, its field was constructed from two pieces of dark blue silk sewn together horizontally, the upper piece being 20" deep and the lower piece 17" deep. The obverse contained a gold painted crescent in the upper staff corner. There is a gold painted palmetto measuring 18" in height in the center of the field, with the date July 21, 1861, painted in black ¾" letters and numerals across its 8"-wide base. Captions above and below the tree are in 2¾" gold block letters, shaded black low and right.

The reverse design simply consists of the inscription, PRESENTED/TO/THE PEE DEE RIFLES/BY/THE LADIES AT HOME/1861, in six lines, all of gold block letters, respectively 2", 1¾", 2¾", 2", 2", and 2" high, with BY and 1861 in Roman uncial letters. The flag is edged on three sides with 1" gold metallic fringe.

The flag is in fragmentary condition today.

South Carolina Confederate Relic Room & Museum, Columbia, S.C.

Union District Volunteers

Co. E, 1st Regiment Infantry, South Carolina Volunteers

Before the Union District Volunteers left for Charleston on January 12, 1861, an unsuccessful attempt was made by a group of local ladies to present them with a flag. An article in the *Unionville Times* explained that:

> "... the ladies of Union, wishing to manifest their appreciation of the conduct of your noble company, by presenting a handsome flag, and knowing their inability to procure suitable materials and make one, ere you go, would beg that you accept the enclosed sum (sixty dollars) and purchase one in Charleston.

> "They propose that it be made of Mazarine blue silk, edged with gold fringe. On one side a Palmetto, with the State arms, with 'Union District Volunteers' in a curve over, and "January 12th, 1861", in a line under it. On the other side, a Star in gold, protected by a drawn Sword, Motto - 'Our Rights, against a World in Arms.' They submit this, giving . . . the privilege of improving it."

The beautiful blue silk banner purchased by the Volunteers through this donation measured 35" (hoist) x 47" (fly).

Chicago Historical Society, Chicago, Illinois

Monticello Guards/ Fairfield Volunteers

Company I, 1ˢᵗ Regiment Infantry, South Carolina Volunteers

The **Monticello Guards/Fairfield Volunteers** were raised in Fairfield District in response to the call for six-month volunteers. John B. Davis was elected captain. Only thirty-two out of eighty men volunteered to finish their six months in Virginia. The ones who stayed served out their time on Morris Island and then left for home on April 26, 1861. In July, when Gregg returned to raise another regiment, the Monticello Guards volunteered but were not accepted. In September 1861, they were mustered into service as Company E, 15ᵗʰ South Carolina Volunteers (DeSaussure's).

After their departure for Virginia, the company was presented with the above flag, possibly made by artist August Knorr. It is 44³/₄" (hoist) x 59" (fly). It is dark blue silk bordered on four sides by a narrow white silk border. The elaborate design is entirely handpainted.

The reverse is similar, with some changes. The three-part ribbon is blue with red borders and bears the inscription VENI/VIDI/VICI in similar lettering. The hanging banner on the reverse is green, also framed in gold fringe. In place of the flag, the panel on the reverse displays a palmetto tree in natural colors.

South Carolina Confederate Relic Room & Museum, Columbia, S.C.

Saluda Guards

Company O, 1st Regiment Infantry, S.C. Volunteers

Through their brief tenure in Confederate service the **Saluda Guards** had three flags, all white. The first was crudely made of white cotton in the form of a banner. It measured 35" (top edge) x 48¼", with no fringe and no apparent method of attachment. A palmetto tree, 22¼" high, is crudely painted in watercolor in the center of the obverse.

Above the tree are stenciled the words SALUDA GUARDS. The first and last letters of each word are 4" high. The others are 1½" high. Below the palmetto in four lines are the words 1861/PRESENTED BY/THE LADIES OF/LEXINGTON, also stenciled and all 1¾" high.

South Carolina Confederate Relic Room & Museum, Columbia, S.C.

Saluda Guards

Company O, 1ˢᵗ Regiment Infantry, S.C. Volunteers

By May 10, 1861, the **Saluda Guards,** also known as the *Saluda Grays,* were designated Company O, 1ˢᵗ South Carolina Volunteers. At the end of their six-month obligation, the company returned to South Carolina. The *Columbia Tri-Weekly Guardian* announced that they "expected to join Gregg's Regiment" for further service.

A third flag, in the collection of the Chicago Historical Society, may have been made under the expectations of the company's rejoining their regiment, a tran-

fer that apparently never transpired. It is made in banner style, with an overhead method of attachment (See *Kings Mountain Guards).* It is 40" (along the sides) x 48" (along the top). It is edged on the bottom and sides with a 6" gold fringe. Centered on the obverse is a 30"-high palmetto tree painted in natural colors. In the upper left is a circle of six gold painted stars surrounding a center star. All of the stars are 2½" diameter. In the top right corner is a 7" diameter gold painted crescent. The unit name is painted underneath the tree in 1¾" pink Roman uncial letters outlined in red. 1861 is in ½" numerals.

Centered on the reverse is a wreath of green rice surrounding the four-line phrase, *Guard this/till our Country's free/Guard it-/and God will prosper thee,* in black painted italicized letters. The capitals are 1¼", and the lowercase letters are ¾" high. A red two-piece scroll displays the words PRESENTED BY THE/LADIES OF LEXINGTON in 1¼" black block letters.

Chicago Historical Society, Chicago, Ill.

Hampton Legion
South Carolina Volunteers

The following excerpt from the *Richmond Daily Dispatch* of July 18, 1861, describes the presentation ceremony in which the Hampton Legion was formally presented with their new colors.

The Legion was formed into three sides of a square to receive the President, who appeared on a grey horse, accompanied by Col. Hampton and staff . . . Advancing a few paces in the hollow of the square, he took the beautiful banner with evident emotion, and addressed his " . . . friends and fellow soldiers of South Carolina . . . and committed the . . . flag in the hands of Col. Hampton . . . Three times three were enthusiastically given for Jeff. Davis, and after the [Armory] Band had played a fine air, Col. Hampton . . . asked them to . . . 'look upon its Palmetto tree and silver crescent.'–then turning to Sergeant [A. Elliott] Darby, he said: 'To you I commit this sacred trust. I know you well—you must remember that you are the grandson of a patriot and a hero'."

On taking it, Sergeant Darby remarked that " . . . it was his pride and pleasure to be the bearer of that beautiful banner . . ."

Every eye rested fondly on the silver crescent and memory moving Palmetto, as the gorgeous flag floated first over the heads of the Legion . . .

[Note: the grandfather of Sgt. Darby was Sergeant William Jasper, the hero of the battle on Sullivan's Island in June 1776. When the state colors were shot down, Sgt. Jasper risked his own life under fire from the enemy to raise the colors above the fort.]

One soldier remembered that the flag "was made of Satin doubled (I think one side was made from Mrs. Preston's wedding dress at least we were under this impression) one side blue and the other side solfereno. A palmetto tree was worked on one side with a crescent, and on the other side a wreath inside of which was Hampton Legion all embroidered in different colors from the flag. The border was gold fringe very heavy at least four inches long. The flag was large enough almost to cover one side of a small "A" tent. It was so large that but few men could handle it properly."

A number of bearers shared the duty at the battle of 1st Manassas, Sgt. Darby leading the charge, being spelled by Lieutenant G.W. Lester, then Corporal O'Conner, in whose hands the flag was when it was waved over a captured Union battery of guns. O'Conner recalled, "I had the honor of bearing our banner, when we captured the celebrated [Sherman's] battery. My gun is torn up, and I escaped almost miraculously."

After 2nd Manassas, Lt. Col. Gary reported, "The colors of the Legion were the first that were planted upon a battery of four guns . . . Sergt. J.H. Satterfield, the color-bearer, was wounded. Never was a flag borne with more dashing courage than he displayed, as the bullet rent folds of the flag will attest." Other reports attest to the fact that the flag was peppered with holes "from edge to edge" with enemy fire.

This flag was carried in all subsequent actions of the Legion until after Sharpsburg, when it was sent home for repairs. It was returned, with some battle honors embroidered, and kept until after Will's Valley, when it was returned to General Hampton for safekeeping.

This flag survived the war but was destroyed in a fire at General Hampton's residence in 1876.

Hampton Legion

South Carolina Volunteers

A second flag, of 1ˢᵗ National pattern, was presented to the **Hampton Legion** by Major Conner at Camp Lee, Bacon Race, Virginia, on November 20, 1861. Made by the "ladies of Matanzas [Cuba]," this flag was brought through the blockade by Captain John N. Maffitt, commanding the *Theodora*.

The *Charleston Daily Courier* of November 30, 1861, recorded the following report from the purser of the *Theodora*.

"Our captain was presented with a beautiful silk flag by the ladies of Havana. The flag was presented by Mrs. L.B. Norris. She delivered a fine speech, and the Captain, on receiving the flag, gave a short but patriotic response."

Two days later the same newspaper reported "The beautiful Confederate flag, lately presented in Havana to the steamer which safely landed our Ministers, SLIDELL and MASON in Cuba, was unfurled yesterday from the flagstaff of the *Courier* office."

Upon arrival in Virginia in a neat case, it was described as "a beautiful Confederate flag—the stars and bars—made of elegant silk, and exhibits exquisite workmanship." This flag was on display at a barbecue held in Columbia on April 22, 1864, being described as "a superb silk banner" suspended over the speaker's stand.

South Carolina Confederate Relic Room & Museum, Columbia, S.C.

Washington Light Infantry
Company A, Infantry Battalion, Hampton Legion

James H. Ancrum, Jr., the color bearer of the **Washington Light Infantry Volunteers,** designed this flag. His sister, Miss M.H. Ancrum, made the banner, aided by Sisters from the Academy of our Lady of Mercy in Charleston. Colonel T.Y. Simonton presented it, on behalf of the ladies, at the Institute Hall in Charleston.

The *Charleston Mercury* described it, saying,

> *"The field conforms in design to the State or Palmetto flag, the ground being of rich and heavy silk. The Palmetto and Crescent are blazoned in silver spangles and white silk, as blended to produce a dazzling effect. The reverse has a ground of white silk, in the middle of which is cunningly embroidered, in natural colors, leaves of laurel and oak intertwined into a beautiful wreath. Within the wreath is a single star, while above appear, in glittering capitals, the words - 'PRO ARIS ET FOCIS.'* [Latin for "For Our Altars and Firesides]. *The staff and mountings of the flag are correspondingly elaborate and striking."*

Mr. R.W. Gale made the staff and flag cover.

Just prior to 1st Manassas, orders were issued for companies to leave their flags at Richmond or send them home. This directive was met with outrage from the men, who according to Captain Conner, "had set their hearts on carrying the flag into the fight." Captain Conner did not want to leave the flag in storage. He wrote to his mother that he intended to leave it at a private house.

It is not known what became of the flag after it left the company.

Claremont Rifles

Company G, Infantry Battalion, Hampton Legion

The **Claremont Rifles** were raised in Stateburg, S.C., in the Claremont region of Sumter District. They served with the 2nd S.C. Regiment on Morris Island during the bombardment of Fort Sumter. When four companies of the regiment were transferred to Virginia, the Claremont Rifles returned to Stateburg and were later incorporated into the Hampton Legion.

Upon organization, Dr. Nelson Burgess presented this flag to the company. It is 34" (hoist) x 36" (fly) and its white silk field is edged on three sides with a 2$^3/_8$"-deep gold metallic fringe. Centered on the obverse is a 16$^1/_2$" tall palmetto tree embroidered in natural colors. Arched above and below the tree in 1$^1/_2$" gold, silk, block letters is the motto WHERE HONOR, LIBERTY/AND OUR STATE CALLS. Centered on the reverse is a 10"-diameter gold embroidered star, edged with a double row of sequins. Arched above the star in letters similar to those on the front is the unit name, CLAREMONT RIFLES. Below the star is the date JANUARY 1861.

South Carolina Confederate Relic Room & Museum, Columbia, S.C.

German Volunteers
Company H, Infantry Battalion, Hampton Legion
Company B, Artillery Battalion, Hampton Legion

"The [company] having been mustered in the Confederate service for the war left Charleston, S.C. on Sept. 10th, 1861—and on the way to the train which was to take the company to Virginia made a stop at the hall where the ordinance of Secession was passed and received a beautiful Guidon which was presented by Gen. J.A. Wagner on behalf of the noble German women of Charleston. The Guidon was received by Capt. W.K. Bachman and by him turned over to the color bearer, Anton W. Jager, who had been selected to carry it.

"The Guidon was of heavy silk, surrounded by gold fringe and was 20 x 28 inches in size. On one side were the German colors, black, red, and gold—with the letters G.V. embroidered in the center with yellow silk outlined into gold thread [G.V. not on surviving flag]. The reverse, the Confederate flag with eleven stars embroidered with white silk on the blue and outlined onto silver thread. The Guidon remained with the company until the spring of 1862, when it became necessary to substitute for it the regular battle flag of the Confederacy [see Artillery section, entry for Bachmann's Battery flag]. The original Guidon is in possession of Capt. W.K. Bachman. The battle flag was given to the color bearer, Anton W. Jager, who carefully kept it until the surrender at Greensboro, North Carolina, in 1865. The faithful color bearer, brought it away around his body and preserves it as a very sacred relic. He resides in Charleston and is greatly esteemed as a good citizen and a gallant survivor. This flag came with the Battery on its return to South Carolina when it was stationed on the line of defense of the Charleston & Savannah R.R. and was carried into North Carolina until the end of the war at Greensboro, N.C. It has inscribed upon its folds the names of many of the great battles of the war. Such as 2nd Manassas, Sharpsburg, Fredericksburg, and others, commencing with the seven days fights in front of Richmond through to Gettysburg besides many minor engagements before and afterwards."

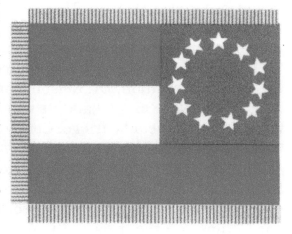

Capt. & Mrs. Bachman, April 1900

Confederate Museum, Charleston, S.C.

South Carolina Zouave Volunteers
Company H (2nd), Infantry Battalion, Hampton Legion

On October 22, 1861, the *Daily Southern Guardian* announced "the flag designed to be presented by the ladies of Columbia to Capt. McCord's Zouave Volunteers will be on exhibition at J.J. Browne's store, next to the Exchange Bank, for a few days." A week later the presentation was made, on which occasion the company, escorted by the Chicora Rifles and the College Cadets, formed in front of the piazza of the Congaree House, where President Longstreet, of the South Carolina College, committed the flag to the care of color bearer, William G. Gardner. Although this flag has not survived, a contemporary description indicates that it was made from blue silk. A white silk palmetto and crescent, embroidered by "the Nuns of Columbia," decorated the obverse side, while the reverse featured a tiger's head, painted by "Monseiur Dovilliers, of Columbia." The pattern for the latter may have been taken from a woodcut used in both Charleston Zouave Cadet and South Carolina Zouave Volunteer company orders published in Charleston and Columbia newspapers in 1861.

This flag did not survive the war.

Edgefield Hussars

Company A, Cavalry Battalion, Hampton Legion

The **Edgefield Hussars** were formed in the wake of South Carolina's Nullification Crisis. Organized in 1833 under Captain Andrew Pickens Butler, by 1851 they were part of the Edgefield Squadron, 2nd Regiment of Cavalry, South Carolina Militia. On January 23, 1861, the company volunteered for state service. On May 8, 1861, the company was received into Confederate service for one year as part of the Hampton Legion. They were led by Captain Matthew Calbraith Butler. When the legion was reorganized on August 22, 1862,

the *Edgefield Hussars* became Company I, 2nd South Carolina Cavalry.

The company's flag is 34½" (hoist) x 40½" (fly) and is made of two thicknesses of blue silk over a cotton center. It is bordered on three sides with a ¼" gold border, to which is attached a 1½" gold fringe. Centered on the obverse is a full-color, embroidered palmetto tree, 21½" tall. In an arch above the tree is SOUTH CAROLINA in 1¾" embroidered block letters. In a reverse arch below the tree is the unit name.

Oakley Park, Red Shirt Shrine, Edgefield, S.C.

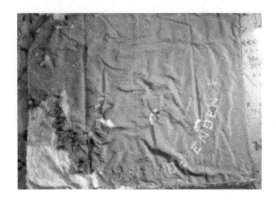

The reverse is very deteriorated and is barely readable. Centered on the reverse is a 3½" six-pointed star embroidered in gold metallic thread. Arched above the star is the motto STATE SOVEREIGNTY. Below the star in a reverse arch is the motto EQUALITY OR INDEPENDENCE.

Beaufort District Troop
Company C, Cavalry Battalion, Hampton Legion

Shortly after they were accepted into the Legion, the **Beaufort District Troop** was presented with this bunting flag. It measured 57" (hoist) by 86" (fly). Included in the fly dimension was a $1^{7}/_{8}$" white canvas hoist with a whipped eyelet at each end. Eleven white cotton five-pointed stars, measuring $5^{3}/_{4}$" from point to point, were randomly scattered over the rectangular blue canton.

It must be assumed that the makers of these banners took pride in their work, sometimes to the point of embroidering their own names on the flag of their making. If we accept this premise, then we must question the seemingly haphazard pattern of star placement. It must be remembered that the Confederate States of America was not "one nation" but a confederation of nation/states. The symbolism of the above pattern (and also that of the Hampton Legion's 1st National) could be a statement that each state was not simply a part of a circle, or union, but free, independent, and sovereign. If that hypothesis is incorrect, then that leaves us with the possibility that the above is truly an unattractive, haphazard arrangement of stars.

The three horizontal bars measured 20", 17", and 20" respectively in depth, and were reinforced in the two corners where the field joins the heading.

South Carolina Confederate Relic Room & Museum, Columbia, S.C.

The Unfolding of the Battle Flag

After the initial conflicts between the two armies, it was found that in the field and in the dust and smoke of battle, the First National was easily confused as the flag of the enemy. A flag specifically for battle was requested. In the eastern theater, General Pierre G. T. Beauregard, commander of the Confederate Army of the Potomac, championed the idea of a new battle flag. In September 1861, he proposed that a design that William Porcher Miles had submitted to Congress as a national flag be adopted as a battle flag.

Miles' design was a rectangular red field traversed by a blue St. Andrew's cross bearing white stars equal in number to the seven states then represented in the Confederate Congress. Beauregard discussed the matter with departmental commander General Joseph E. Johnston, and the design was adopted. In its final version the flag was made square to conserve cloth, and a protective border was added.

To the Cary cousins of Richmond, Virginia, was given the honor of making the first samples. Constance Cary Harrison remembered in her diary:

> Another incident of note, during the autumn of '61, was that to my cousins, Hettie and Jennie Cary, and to me was entrusted the making of the first three battle flags of the Confederacy. They were jaunty squares of scarlet crossed with dark blue edged with white, the cross bearing stars to indicate the number of the seceded States. We set our best stitches upon them, edged them with golden fringes, and when they were finished, dispatched one to Johnston, another to Beauregard, and the third to Earl Van Dorn, then commanding infantry at Manassas. The banners were received with all possible enthusiasm; we were toasted, feted, and cheered abundantly.

After a few battle flags of this design had been made for presentation, the Confederate quartermaster ordered 120 for the Army of Northern Virginia. They were fabricated of dress silk and were made by Richmond sewing circles.

One South Carolina battle flag with ties to the Cary cousins is that of *Captain Charles' Battery of Light Artillery.*

Any attempt to arrange anything Confederate in uniform categories usually meets with classification frustration. The term "Confederate uniform" is often used as an explanation for the word "oxymoron," insinuating, of course, that the adjective "Confederate" is synonymous with irregularity or inconsistency. The same nonconformity of standards is met when one attempts to classify or categorize the different issues of the Army of Northern Virginia battle flag.

For over a hundred years, vexillologists have attempted, with measurements, diagrams, and tables, to differentiate among the periodic disbursements of flags that emanated from the Richmond Depot throughout the war, with varying results. The one issue on which most flag "experts" agree is the 1st (Silk) Pattern.

1st (Silk) Pattern: Autumn 1861

The first battle flag samples were made by the Cary cousins and other ladies of the Richmond sewing circles. The first General Issue flags were made by Richmond ladies under government contract according to the patterns of the samples. Their blue crosses were eight inches wide, edged with three-quarter-inch fimbriation made of white silk. The twelve stars were four and one-half inches in diameter and set eight inches apart from the center of the cross. The presentation flags of this issue sported gold fringe on three sides. For field use, to save on cost, and perhaps to simulate the gold of the fringe, the edges were bound in yellow silk. The hoist had a silk sleeve. An interesting characteristic of these flags came from the choice of materials and manufacture. For obvious Victorian reasons, ladies of the South did not often wear red dresses. So despite the fact that the first samples were "jaunty squares of scarlet," there was not enough red silk in Richmond to outfit an army. Due to lack of this color material, the flags issued to the troops tended to be pinkish rather than scarlet. Remaining flags of this issue, notably the flag of the 6th S.C. Regiment, are faded nearly white. Other flags of this type were issued to the 4th S.C. Regiment and the Palmetto Sharpshooters.

Army of Northern Virginia: Cotton Issue

The Cotton Issue battle flags appear to have been experimental and issued in conjunction with the above-mentioned silk issue. They were only issued to four brigades in the Virginia theater. Since they were attached to Wigfall's/Hood's brigade, it is possible that the Hampton Legion was issued one of the cotton battle flags. If they did receive one, it did not survive the war. The acceptance of this issue as a separate category has caused confusion in establishing the chronology of the battle flag. If one accepts the Cotton Issue as a separate disbursement, the 1st Bunting Issue (discussed next) becomes the 2nd Bunting Issue. For the purpose of this work, since the Cotton Issue does appear to be experimental, and there is no known surviving South Carolina example, it will not be considered as a separate issue.

1st Bunting Issue: Early 1862

These were similar to the first silk pattern flags but made of wool bunting, with a true scarlet field. Instead of yellow silk, the edgings were made with orange flannel, one and one-half inches wide. In the field, the orange soon faded to yellow and the yellow to tan. The edging color is not easily discernible on surviving examples. The thirteenth star was added at the center of the cross, and the cotton stars were smaller, only three inches in diameter. They were set six inches apart from the center of the cross, giving the stars an appearance of being compressed toward the center. The fimbriation was made of one-half-inch-wide cotton. The staff side was made with a two-inches-wide white cotton canvas or linen hoist with three whipped eyelets for ties.

It would appear that the Malvern Hill Flag is of the 1st Bunting Issue.

2nd Bunting Issue: Spring 1862

The 2nd Bunting Issue was slightly changed. With this issue, the width of the blue cross was reduced from eight inches to five inches to conserve stocks of blue cloth. Despite these conservation efforts, the depot soon used up its supplies of red and blue wool and orange flannel. Later flags of this issue were made with cloth run through the blockade. The stars remained small, three and three-quarters inches in diameter, and were arranged close to the flag's center, maintaining the compressed appearance.

The flags of the 2nd S.C. Regiment and 21st S.C. Regiment are good examples of the 2nd Bunting Issue flags.

3rd Bunting Issue: 1862 - 1864

In July 1862, the Richmond Depot began production of the third and largest issue of Army of Northern Virginia battle flags. The most noticeable difference is the change from orange borders to white borders. These flags were made until May of 1864, in quantities that allowed issue to entire divisions at a time. D.H. Hill's division received new colors after Fredericksburg, A.P. Hill's after Chancellorsville, and several commands that had lost heavily in colors were given replacements after Gettysburg.

Irregularities in construction and application of battle honors cause flags of the 3rd Bunting Issue to look quite dissimilar. Some honors are applied in white paint, some in blue, and some in black. Some are applied in a circular pattern while others are applied in all horizontal text. Some 3rd Issue flags never had honors applied. The one common feature is the white border.

This white-bordered battle flag is commonly referred to today as the battle flag despite the many gold-bordered flags that went before it. This acceptance could be in part due to its adoption in 1905 by the United Confederate Veterans as their official flag. (In later reunion photographs, however, the veterans actually seem to have preferred the rectangular Army of Tennessee version of the battle flag.)

Some examples of South Carolina flags of the 3rd Bunting Issue are the 3rd S.C. Regiment and the 8th S.C. Regiment.

Note: There is no single "correct" orientation for stars on a South Carolina battle flag. It appears that the stars were sewn onto the blue bars prior to final assembly. The orientation of the star, shown by whether one ray points up or down, depends on how the blue bar was sewn into the flag. On the flag of the 5th Cavalry, captured at Trevilian Station, the stars on three bars point upward while the stars on one bar point down. In the flag of the 7th Regiment Infantry, the stars point alternately up and down. Very few battle flags show all of the stars pointing in one direction.

2ⁿᵈ Regiment Infantry
South Carolina Volunteers

    The **2ⁿᵈ S.C. Infantry Regiment** was organized under a state legislative act of December 17, 1860, which called for the formation of ten 12-month regiments for the defense of the state. The 2ⁿᵈ Regiment was enlisted under the command of Colonel Joseph B. Kershaw and remained with Kershaw's brigade for the duration of the war.

    This battle flag of the 2ⁿᵈ S.C. Regiment is 48" (hoist) x 48¼" (fly). It appears to have been the color issued prior to the adoption of battle flags by Kershaw's brigade bearing battle honors, which were issued to the entire brigade after Chancellorsville. This flag was probably pressed back into service after the loss of the unit's flag at Cedar Creek, Virginia, on October 19, 1864 (War Dept. capture No. 185).

    Samuel Gaillard Pinkney saved this flag from capture at the end of the war.

The Citadel Museum, Charleston, S.C.

Palmetto Guard

South Carolina Militia/South Carolina Volunteers

This richly embroidered blue silk flag of the Palmetto Guard is 34" (hoist) x 42" (fly). Centered on the obverse is a naturally colored palmetto tree, 19" tall and 9¾" wide at its widest branches. In a flowing arch above the tree, in 1⅞" block letters, is the motto FORTIS CADERE CEDERE NON POTEST.

Sequined letters

The motto above the palmetto tree and the date below are fabricated from individually applied gold sequins attached with gold thread and laid out in two-wide rows. The letters in the motto are 1⅞" tall, while the letters in the date are 1⅝" tall.

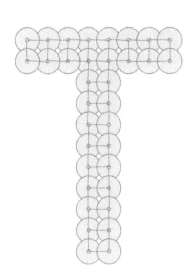

Displayed with the flag of the Palmetto Guard is the following letter.

This flag was broaidered and made and prepared by the hands of some of the Fair Daughters of South Carolina friends of the Palmetto Guard, Capt. Geo. B. Cuthbert commanding. Thus panoplied and accieded at their command, the Palmetto Guard went to war, a war which in the last analysis was a war of self defense. We find that the civilization of the day will not tolerate any other and yet ___!!! However it has been recognized that the states were strictly within their rights when they seceded from the United States. Hence, coersion even offensive aggression. Hence the states acted strictly right when they resisted the aggression.

In this war when this flag of our fair friends in the hands of the Palmetto Guard entered to repell invasion. It certainly did accomplish its purpose victoriously. It drove the invaders back in tumultuous rout. It never suffered defeat after this great triumph. For the authorities determined that it was inexpedient to use any flags other than Regimental flags. So this our victorious flag with its three bullet holes left in it by the invaders was sent to South Carolina.

So this is our flag of Victory. As the wingless victory may it always remain with you.

R. Heber Screvens
Col. Charleston
Regiment

Confederate Museum,
Charleston, S.C.

Centered on the reverse is a 24"-diameter wreath, embroidered in natural colors, the left side being of magnolia leaves and berries, the right being of oak leaves and acorns. The letters and numbers are fully embroidered with metallic golden thread.

3rd Regiment Infantry
South Carolina Volunteers

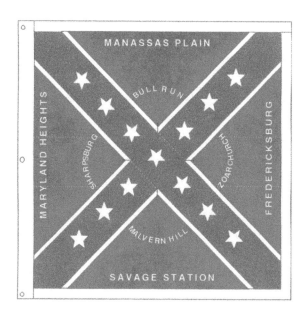

The **3rd Regiment S.C. Infantry** was assembled in April 1861, in Columbia. The regiment fought at 1st Manassas in Brigadier General Milledge Bonham's brigade, but for the war it is associated with Brigadier General Joseph B. Kershaw's brigade.

The 47¼" (hoist) x 45½" (fly) flag was issued in 1862 and was brought home by the veterans. Battle honors are painted in white stylized Gothic letters, the larger being 2½" high and the smaller being 1¾" high. Those in the fly quadrant are extremely faint; those in the lower quadrant are completely obliterated. Based on the flag of the *8th Regiment*, it could be that two honors were in the lower quadrant: MALVERN HILL in the inner circle, and SAVAGE STATION along the bottom edge. Their last fight was at Bentonville, North Carolina. The 3rd Regiment had 563 wartime deaths.

This flag was given to the State of South Carolina by the veterans of the Regiment on February 2, 1925 (See the article from *The State*, included with the entry on the flag of the 10th Regiment). At this ceremony, the flag was presented by Representative James A. Sullivan of Laurens, speaking on behalf of O.G. Thompson of Laurens, one of the Regiment's few survivors.

South Carolina Confederate Relic Room & Museum, Columbia, S.C.

Williams Guards

Company B, 3rd Regiment Infantry, South Carolina Volunteers

"On the 5th day of January, 1861, at Jalapa, South Carolina, the Williams Guards was organized. The Company was known as Company B, 3rd Regiment, S.C.V. It was part of the 1st Brigade, 1st Division, Army of Northern Virginia.

"The Company engaged in all the principal fights in Virginia. After the Battle of Gettysburg, two divisions of Longstreet's corps, Hood's and McLaws', were transferred to the Army of the West (Army of Tennessee). Company B was part of McLaws' Division and, of course, was transferred to the Western Army. The Company took part in the battles of Chickamauga, Knoxville, and Bean Station.

"In 1864 it was sent back to Virginia and was made part of Lee's army, and so remained until Sherman took possession of Savannah. The Company surrendered with Johnston at Greensboro, N.C. (on) April 26, 1865.

"A short time after the organization of the Company, Mrs. James McCravey presented the Company a flag. The Company left Newberry on the 13th day of April, and was in camp at the fairgrounds in Columbia for some time. While in Columbia, another flag was presented by Mrs. Trezevant. Soon after the Company moved to Lightwood Knot Springs to join the Army of Northern Virginia sometime in June 1861.

"It was soon found that the Company had no use for the flags, so Captain Samuel Newton Davidson sent the flags home to his sister, Mrs. Mary F. Reeder, to keep until the Company should return home.

"Mr. W.G. Peterson, sergeant of the Company, on return to his home, along with his comrades after the War was over, began to make inquiries as to these Company flags. It was natural that the survivors of the Company should desire the possession of these flags.

"The following statement of facts in connection with the flags is made by Mr. Peterson:

'After the surrender, Mrs. Reeder moved to McCormick, S.C. during the (blank), I got in correspondence with Mrs. Reeder about the flags. She finally turned them over to me in trust for the Company, and I let Captain Thompson Connor, Sergeant A.J. Livingston and M.H. Gary know that I had the flags. We decided to put the flags in the hands of the senior ranking officer of the Company, in trust for the survivors until the survivors decided what was to be done with them. I at once turned them over to Connor in trust for the Company.

'At Captain Connor's death, Mrs. Connor asked me what she was to do with the flags. I instructed her to turn them over to Sergeant L.M. Speers in trust for the Company. She turned them over to Speers with full explanation about what was to be done with them. Mr. Speers did not know until that time what had become of the flags. Mrs. Speers and I talked the matter over very frequently.'

"The Company desires that these Flags shall be placed in the Relic Room in Columbia, and desires also that the presentation of them shall be made in behalf of the Company through the Drayton Rutherford Chapter, Daughters of the Confederacy.

" . . .Those who do survive . . .desire to place these Company flags in the custody of the State, and . . .properly cared for by the authorities of the State."

From original in the Relic Room by "Survivors of the Company."

Both flags of the Williams Guards are in the collection of the South Carolina Confederate Relic Room & Museum, Columbia, S.C.

Laurens Briars

Co. G, 3rd Regiment Infantry, South Carolina Volunteers

The **Laurens Briars** were mustered into Confederate service on June 6, 1861, as Company G, 3rd Regiment Infantry, South Carolina Volunteers. Their first commander was Captain R.P. Todd.

By October of that year they were in Winchester, Virginia. On December 13, 1863, the *Briars* fought the enemy at Fredericksburg. The company lost four men killed, the Captain and five men severely wounded, and five more men wounded slightly. They spent the winter at Fredericksburg.

That summer they marched on the Gettysburg campaign and in the fall went with General Longstreet to Tennessee. In December, they were in camp near Russellsville, Tennessee.

Returning to Virginia, they took part in the many battles of the Richmond campaign. Written in the company records is the statement that the company "fought at Wilderness, Spottsylvania, N. Anna and Cold Harbor and *acted well*."

The flag of the *Laurens Briars* is 34" (hoist) x 40" (fly) and is bordered on three sides with 2" gold fringe.

South Carolina Confederate Relic Room & Museum, Columbia, S.C.

THE FLAGS OF CIVIL WAR SOUTH CAROLINA

4th Regiment Infantry
South Carolina Volunteers

Before the **4th Infantry Regiment** left for Virginia, a correspondent for an Anderson newspaper suggested that the wealthy citizens of Anderson, Pickens, and Greenville should provide a flag for the regiment. The *Keowee Courier* of March 9, 1861, suggested that the ladies of the district should produce the flag. The richly embroidered flag shown above is apparently the result of this campaign.

This 1st National flag was brought home to South Carolina from the war by Captain John Hallums Bowen and has since remained in the possession of his descendants. The flag is 42" (hoist) x 62¼" (fly). Each panel is made of two layers of very finely woven wool. The blue canton is 28" square. On the obverse is a

white, embroidered palmetto tree, 12½" high and 7½" wide. The unit name, 4th REGT, is embroidered in an arch above the palmetto in 3"-high Roman uncial letters. In a reverse arch below the tree are the letters S.C.V. in 3½" Roman uncials. The crescent is 6" point to point. The three bars are from top to bottom 13½", 14½", and 14" respectively.

In the canton on the reverse is an 18½" diameter circle of eleven stars. The stars have a diameter of 3½". In the center of the circle of stars is the unit designation 4th REGT/S.C.V.

The number 4 is 3¾" high while the letters R,E, and G are 3" high. The letters S,C, and V are 4" high. All are fully embroidered block letters.

The flag is in good condition. There is some damage at the top of the hoist corner and some repairs made in the canton. There are a number of small holes in the flag, some of which may be bullet holes.

The 4th Regiment, under the command of General Nathan "Shanks" Evans, was in the thick of the fight at the First Battle of Manassas and were among the first to respond to the Union flanking movement. Due to bat-

tle deaths and illness, the regiment was reorganized the following April and served with the Hampton Legion as the 4th Battalion.

In the possession of a descendant of Captain John Hallums Bowen.

4th Regiment Infantry
South Carolina Volunteers

On July 4, 1861, at "Camp Carolina," near Leesburg, Virginia, Lieutenant Colonel Charles Binn Tebbs, of the 8th Virginia Volunteers, presented the 4th South Carolina Regiment with "an elegant Confederate Flag." This flag was presented on behalf of "the ladies of Leesburg." Made of merino wool, it was described as being of "regimental size," but at 84" (hoist) x 132" (fly), it was rather larger than a regimental color. Private William Steele (Co. K) indicated in his diary that it was a "neat garrison flag." This is confirmed by a newspaper account of it being "hoisted on a tall liberty pole in front of the camp." Of First National pattern, its dark blue canton displayed eleven appliqued five-pointed stars arranged with six in a circle, one in the center, and one at each corner. It was attached to the staff by a white cotton sleeve, approximately 4" wide, and was edged on three sides with ¼"-wide dark blue cotton binding.

On November 28, 1861, the regiments of Longstreet's Division were presented new 1ˢᵗ issue silk flags. J.W. Reid of Co. C, 4ᵗʰ Regt. recalled:

Thursday Evening, Nov. 28ᵗʰ—

The biggest day yet. This morning at 10.30 o'clock everybody and the cook was called out, and each regiment was presented with a battle flag. General Beauregard was present and so was everybody else. It was the grandest time we have ever had. We were told that the flags were made and sent to us by our wives, mothers, and sisters with an order from them to defend them. There were several bands of music on hand, and as each regiment filed off toward their quarters, every band struck up "Pop Goes the Weasel." . . . . The noise of the men was deafening.

Neither of the above flags has survived the war. Some fragments of the silk battle flag are at the S.C. Confederate Relic Room.

5ᵗʰ Regiment Infantry
South Carolina Volunteers

The **5ᵗʰ South Carolina Regiment** was formed in April 1861, and was mustered into Confederate service on June 4, 1861. When the first year's enlistments expired, the regiment disbanded. Colonel Jenkins went on to form the Palmetto Sharpshooters and the 5ᵗʰ Regiment immediately reorganized under Colonel Asbury Coward.

On November 28, 1861, Anderson's Brigade, along with the rest of Longstreet's Division, received Army of Northern Virginia battle flags. These 1ˢᵗ issue flags were made of silk and were approximately 48" square. They had twelve stars on a St. Andrew's cross. The flag presented to First Sergeant Hugh J. Allison, color bearer of the 5ᵗʰ South Carolina Regiment, has not survived.

The Regiment participated in the battles of Williamsburg and through the Seven Day's fight outside Richmond. It may be assumed that they were given honors similar to other regiments involved, those being WILLIAMSBURG and SEVEN PINES. With the 5ᵗʰ Regiment at the heart of the action at the Battle of Frazier's Farm on June 30, 1862, the flag was struck *30 times* by enemy fire.

Later the regiment was probably given a 3ʳᵈ issue bunting flag.

At the Wilderness, when the color bearer was hit by fire, Colonel Coward carried the colors and advanced ahead of his troops, admonishing his men to follow.

When the Army of Northern Virginia laid down its arms at Appomattox, the men of the 5ᵗʰ Regiment tore the flag to shreds rather than surrender it.

The flag pictured above is a reconstruction. The flag of the 5ᵗʰ S.C. did not survive the war.

Johnson Riflemen

Company A, 5th Regiment Infantry, South Carolina Volunteers

On February 7, 1861, at the Culp House in Unionville, the Johnson Riflemen were presented a flag. This 35" (hoist) x 43" (fly) flag was made by a group of ladies in Unionville and presented to the company by Mr. B.F. Arthur, on behalf of Mrs. Ann Meng Wallace.

This flag is bordered on three sides by 2½" gold silk fringe. Centered on the obverse side is a painted white 5¼" star, above which is arched six smaller 3¾" stars. On either side of the center star are the white Roman uncial letters, J and R. Two sections of a plain-painted red scroll curl around these two letters and join in a knot below the star. These two sections of scroll bear the motto OUR LIBERTIES/DEARER THAN OUR LIVES in ⅝" painted gold block letters. Also in gold, at each of the four corners, is a rococo-style flourish.

On the left of the reverse side is an eagle in flight, painted mainly in shades of brown. In its beak is a red curling scoll with the motto THE/REFUGE OF/AMERICAN LIBERTY in ⅝" gold block letters. On the right side of the reverse is a naturally colored 26"-high palmetto tree with two elliptical shields at its base. The shields bear the obverse and the reverse of the coat of arms of South Carolina on a buff background framed in gold.

Union County Historical Society Museum, Union, S.C.

Pea Ridge Volunteers

Co. B (later Co. E), 5th Regiment Infantry, S.C. Volunteers

The flag of the Pea Ridge Volunteers measures 36" (hoist) x 42½" (fly), and consists of two layers of dark blue silk bound together on three sides with a 1¼" gold metallic fringe. The seal on the obverse is handpainted and depicts a scene at Charleston harbor. The eight stars likely include Virginia, the eighth state to secede, and would date the flag to April 1861.

The reverse field bears a single, large, gold, five-pointed star with an 11⅛" diameter. A three-piece gold scroll edged in black

arches over the star, and contains the motto RESISTANCE/TO TYRANTS IS OBEDIENCE/ TO GOD in crimson block letters, shaded black low and right. A smaller three-piece scroll curves below the star, bearing the inscription PRESENTED/BY THE LADIES/OF UNION, also in crimson block letters shaded in the same manner.

The flag may have seen duty for a short time as the 5th Regimental colors. The flag was sent home to Union, S.C., after the battle of Seven Pines as a covering for the body of slain Lieutenant Edward J. McKissick. Prior to the war, McKissick and Miss Kate Lindsey were sweethearts. Miss Lindsey had actually helped with the preparation of the flag by sewing on the fringe. The flag was kept in the McKissick family until 1904, when McKissick's brother presented it to the city of Union. A great ceremony was held in which the son of Mrs. Thomas McNally (the former Kate Lindsey) sang "Just Before the Battle Mother." Afterwards J.L. Strain made a "ringing speech" and placed the flag in the hands of the William Wallace Chapter U.D.C. and Camp Giles as a sacred trust from the widow and son of one of Union's gallant soldiers, Col. I.G. McKissick.

Union County Historical Society, Union, S.C.

Kings Mountain Guards
Company F, 5th Regiment Infantry

The **Kings Mountain Guards** were enrolled in state service from York County in April 1861, and served throughout the war as Company F, 5th S.C. Volunteer Infantry. They fought with the regiment at 1st Manassas. Twenty-seven men surrendered at Appomattox. Third Sergeant John Knox brought these colors home to South Carolina.

The flag is made of blue silk with a painted 24"-diameter circular seal. It is 36" (hoist) x 38" (fly). The flag is of an unusual early war design with fringe on the left and right sides and on the bottom. This raises questions as to the method of carry. Possible methods are Roman-style on a T-shaped pole, or lancer style with the shaft in a forward charging position, a moot point since it is unlikely that the flag was ever carried in battle.

This flag is in fragile condition, but complete. The seal has many horizontal cracks. The 3" gold fringe is complete. The 1¼" embroidered letters are in gold script, all capitals, reading LIKE OUR ANCESTORS/WE WILL BE FREE.

The flag was a gift from Mrs. C.M. Knox, Jr., of Clover, S.C.

South Carolina Confederate Relic Room & Museum, Columbia, S.C.

Catawba Light Infantry
Company H, 5ᵗʰ Regiment Infantry, South Carolina Volunteers

This flag of the **Catawba Light Infantry** was made by the ladies of Yorkville, and presented to the company in 1861.

The flag is square, 41" x 41" (including fringe). The field is of blue silk, constructed over cotton and handsewn. The obverse displays a 25" oil-painted seal with a scene depicting Charleston harbor. Arched above the seal, in 2" gold silk embroidered letters, is the motto OUR RIGHTS WE DEFEND.

Centered in the reverse of the flag is a 14"-diameter gold five-pointed star with a 1¼" six-pointed star sewn in the center. In a semi-circle around the star, in 2" gold silk embroidered letters, is the company name.

The flag has 2½" gold silk fringe sewn on three sides, with a sleeve attachment on the hoist edge.

This flag is in very fragile condition. The seal is shredding.

Museum of the Confederacy, Richmond, Va.

Palmetto Sharpshooters
(Jenkins Infantry Regiment)
South Carolina Volunteers

The Palmetto Sharpshooters were formed in the spring of 1862 with approximately 1,650 members. Throughout the war, their service was with the Army of Northern Virginia. With Colonel Jenkins' promotion to brigadier general, they served as part of Jenkins' Brigade at Fredericksburg. They accompanied Longstreet to Knoxville, and then returned to Virginia in the spring of 1864. At the surrender at Appomattox, the regiment had 29 commissioned officers and 356 enlisted men.

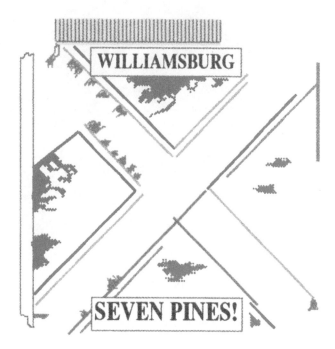

After organization and the trip to Richmond, the local ladies presented a 1st (silk) issue battle flag to the regiment. It was carried into the battle of Seven Pines where, of the entire twelve-man color guard, all but one were killed or wounded. The one who escaped injury, Corporal William Poe, was later killed at Lookout Mountain. The unsurrendered flag was brought back to Pendleton, where it later came into the possession of Pvt. Crayton L. Reid.

The flag suffered severely from battle, time, and the hands of souvenir gatherers as it appeared at reunions of the Regiment's survivors, and was finally reduced to silken shreds.

Nevertheless, the S.C. Confederate Relic Room thought that the symbol under which these brave men fought could and should be presented for the public. The double handful of shredded fabric was laid out and pieced together as a puzzle, framed, and is on display in Columbia.

South Carolina Confederate Relic Room & Museum, Columbia, S.C.

Palmetto Sharpshooters
(Jenkins' Infantry Regiment)
South Carolina Volunteers

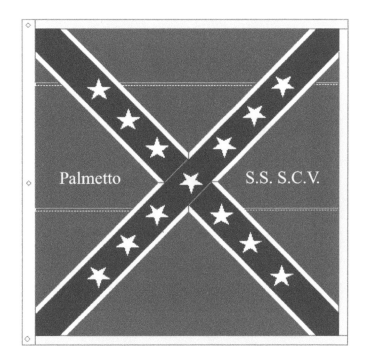

It is unclear when this flag of the **Palmetto Sharpshooters** was captured. It was first in the possession of a Union soldier, John Powell Anderson, who is said to have taken it from the body of a dead Confederate soldier. It was handed down in Anderson's family until purchased by a collector in 1990. Since that time it has been on the collector's market.

Anderson's unit, the 2nd Michigan, engaged or was near the Palmetto Sharpshooters at two occasions, Campbell Station, Tennessee, on November 16, 1863, and the Wilderness in Virginia, in May 1864. It could have been captured at either location.

It is a 3rd bunting issue flag. The unit designation "Palmetto" and "S.S. S.C.V." is painted on in white Roman uncial and miniscule letters, respectively 1$\frac{3}{8}$" and $\frac{3}{4}$" high on the obverse only.

In the possession of a private collector in Pennsylvania.

6th Regiment Infantry
South Carolina Volunteers

The first pattern Army of Northern Virginia battle flags were sewn of dress silk by Richmond ladies under contract. Their blue crosses were 8 inches wide, edged with ³/₄" white silk. The *twelve stars* were 4¹/₂ inches in diameter and set 8 inches apart from the center of the cross. All the edges but the hoist were bound in yellow silk; the hoist had a blue silk sleeve. Finally, the fields tended to be pinkish rather than scarlet.

This first pattern Army of Northern Virginia battle flag was carried by the **6th South Carolina Infantry.** The large block battle honors were the first style produced and were issued to General James Longstreet's troops.

The regiment, part of General David R. Dorn's brigade, received its flag on November 28, 1861, in a ceremony that one soldier in another regiment recalled as "the grandest time we ever had . . . We were drawn up in a hollow square and several speeches were made . . . The noise of the men was deafening."

The flag of the 6th Regiment has been preserved and is on display in Columbia. Its condition is good, but the pink has faded to almost white.

South Carolina Confederate Relic Room & Museum, Columbia, S.C.

7th Regiment Infantry
South Carolina Volunteers

On November 28, 1861, the **7th S.C. Regiment,** being a part of Bonham's Brigade, was presented a silk battle flag. This first issue Army of Northern Virginia flag was carried by the regiment on the Maryland campaign of 1862.

The color bearers of the Army carried with them an awful responsibility. They knew that the eyes of every man in their regiment were fixed upon the color guard. At the center of the regimental line, the colors were a point of reference to maintain the continuity of the attack line. They marked the location of the colonel and his command staff. If the colors were down, it might be assumed that the command structure of the unit was lost. The bearers realized their position and often displayed heroic behavior beyond modern understanding. On December 27, 1862, Colonel Aiken wrote the following letter to the *Southern Guardian* (Columbia) describing the action of his color guard at Maryland Heights.

"When the second halt was ordered, and the men, commanded to lie down, my color sergeant, Charley [Burress], stood erect and kept his colors unfurled. I shouted to him to lie down, but he, believing it his duty to keep our tattered flag aloft, still stood up. I approached and ordered him down. In the act of obeying this last stern command he received a fatal wound in the abdomen. Another member of the color guard, Belton Adams, immediately arose, and catching the falling staff, raised it over his head. In an instant he fell mortally wounded. Before the colors reached the ground they were snatched up by still another member of the color guard, Middleton Quarles, who whirled them over his head, and rushed forward only to meet another messenger of death. Two of my color-guard, Gus. White and L. Coleman, had previously been severely wounded. There being but one remaining, I ordered the colors to be left as they lay, a temporary winding sheet for poor Quarles."

This flag is not known to have survived the war.

7th Regiment Infantry
South Carolina Volunteers

Mrs. Eula Gleaton of Johnston, S.C. wrote:

"My father, B. Wallace Wright, carried this flag home with him from the Battle of Bentonville, N.C. His home was in Edgefield County (now Saluda County). This flag was kept furled in our home for many years, except when unfurled to show someone.

I remember his showing the flag to several friends on one occasion. One of these was Pink (A.P.) Bouknight, who asked to borrow the flag for a Confederate reunion in Johnston, S.C. I think this was about 1925 or 1926. The flag was never returned to my father."

She goes on to recount a brief history of the regiment's service.

"My father was in the Battle of Chancellorsville . . . and the Battle of Fredericksburg . . . Cold Harbor . . . Petersburg . . . and Seven Pines . . . also many others."

Mary B. Poppenheim, a cousin of Lt. A.P. Bouknight of Company M, presented the flag to the Relic Room.

This flag is 48" (hoist) x 51" (fly). The cross is constructed of bars 4³/₄" wide. The stars are 4¹/₂" in diameter, and the eight-inch spacing between stars identifies this flag as a 3rd bunting issue. There are three sewn eyelets along the 2¹/₄" canvas hoist. The pattern of this flag is quite common except for the alternating rotation of the stars, which is quite uncommon.

South Carolina Confederate Relic Room & Museum, Columbia, S.C.

7th Battalion Infantry
South Carolina Volunteers

The **7th Battalion Infantry** was organized with five companies on February 22, 1862. Companies F and G were added on May 27, 1862. Company H was included on October 16, 1862. Their first commander was Lieutenant Colonel Patrick Nelson, and they were often referred to as "Nelson's Battalion." For the most part of the war, they were attached to Hagood's Brigade and took part in the campaigns of that unit.

They were engaged at Edisto Island, Coosawhatchie, and Charleston Harbor. In Virginia they fought at Drewry's Bluff, the siege of Petersburg, Weldon Railroad, and Fort Harrison. They were recalled to the Carolinas to resist Sherman, fought at Bentonville, and surrendered on April 26, 1865.

The blue silk flag shown above is much too fine to be a battle flag. Its construction is elaborate, festooned with sequins and sewn with gold metallic embroidery. It shows little sign of field damage, and was likely used only in ceremonial functions. On the reverse are ten stars formed in the shape of a Christian cross, with six in the upright and two on either side as the arms of the cross. Arched above the cross in gold block letters are the words SURSUM CORGA, and in a reverse arch below, QUID NON PRO PATRIA.

South Carolina Confederate Relic Room & Museum, Columbia, S.C.

7ᵗʰ Battalion Infantry
South Carolina Volunteers

This flag is among three unidentified flags captured from General Johnson Hagood's Brigade at the battle of Weldon Railroad, Virginia, on August 21, 1864. On this date, three commands of this brigade lost their battle flags, all similar and all unmarked. These units were the 7ᵗʰ Battalion, the 21ˢᵗ Regiment, and the 25ᵗʰ Regiment, all South Carolina Volunteers. One of these flags (War Dept. capture no. 154), the one shown above, has a red hoist. This small clue could identify this flag as having belonged to the **7ᵗʰ Battalion, South Carolina Volunteers.**

On the Battalion's ceremonial flag, shown elsewhere in this book, the unit abbreviated its name as "7ᵗʰ S.C. BAT." The flag maker could possibly have confused this abbreviation to stand for "7ᵗʰ Battery," which would explain the red hoist, usually a characteristic of an artillery flag.

The flag is 48" (hoist) x 48" (fly), and is made of red and blue wool. The white edging and 3³/₄" stars spaced 8" apart on 8¹/₂"-wide blue bars identify this flag as a Charleston depot flag, probably issued shortly before the unit's departure for Virginia. The flag is handsewn, with four red quadrants and thirteen evenly spaced stars all with folded hems.

Although the field and the cross are slightly tattered, the flag is listed as being in "good condition."

Museum of the Confederacy, Richmond, Virginia

Malvern Hill Flag

In the ill-fated charge at Malvern Hill, Virginia, General Joseph B. Kershaw's Brigade of South Carolinians did more than their duty, taking fearful losses in their attempt to follow orders. On the evening of July 1, 1862, charging gallantly in the face of overwhelming enemy artillery fire, the brigade lost 164 men out of 956 committed.

Written on this 1st bunting issue battle flag is, *Taken at the Battle of Malven near James River, Virginia, July 1, 1862 by the Butterfield's Brigade, J. Whittick, 83rd Pennsylvania Volunteers. Taken from a South Carolina Regiment who piled up their dead to resist the attack of the Brigade.*

South Carolina Relic Room & Museum, Columbia, S.C.

Kershaw's Brigade at Malvern Hill

2nd S.C. Regt.: Col. J.D. Kennedy
3rd S.C. Regt.: Col. J.D. Nance
7th S.C. Regt.: Col. D.W. Aiken
8th S.C. Regt.: Col. J.W. Henagan
The *23rd S.C. Regiment* was also engaged, but was not part of Kershaw's Brigade.

8th Regiment Infantry
South Carolina Volunteers

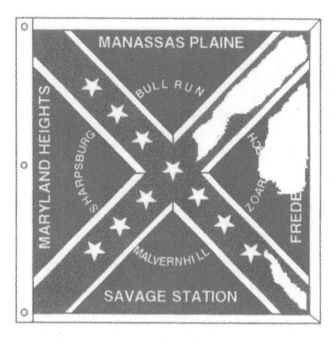

This 3rd bunting issue battle flag of the **8th S.C. Regiment** is 46" square. Battle honors are painted in white stylized Gothic letters, the larger (outer) being 2¼" high and the smaller (inner) being 1¾" high. In the upper quadrant on the reverse of the red field is the single battle honor CHANCELLORSVILLE, painted in white stylized Gothic letters, 2¼" high, reading from fly to staff, opposite MANASSAS PLAINE.

The 8th Regiment served in Kershaw's Brigade, participating in the battles noted on the Regimental colors. Corp. Isaac Gause of Co. E, 2nd Ohio Cavalry, captured these colors on September 13, 1864. On this day, Colonel Henagan, commander of the 8th Regiment, and every member of the regiment were also captured.

On September 13, 1864, the 8th Regiment was on picket duty for Kershaw's Division (at Abraham's Creek near Winchester, Virginia). On this day, the 1st (U.S.) Brigade, 3rd Division of the Cavalry Corps, moved rapidly in, driving the Confederate cavalry before them. With a "sudden dash" of the 3rd N.J. and 2nd Ohio, the 8th Regiment was broken and completely surrounded. The entire regiment, 16 officers and 145 men, was captured, along with its battle flag. Kershaw's troops responded in force but the Union cavalry withdrew from the field, taking with them their prisoners. (OR, Ser. I, Vol. XLIII, Pt. 1, pp. 24, 427, 530)

These colors, War Dept. capture No. 172, were returned by the U.S. War Department in 1905.

South Carolina Confederate Relic Room & Museum, Columbia, S.C.

10ᵗʰ Regiment Infantry
South Carolina Volunteers

After Shiloh, General P.G.T. Beauregard requested reinforcements from the east. In April 1862, two regiments of South Carolina troops, the 10ᵗʰ and the 19ᵗʰ, were assigned to the Army of Mississippi. They fought at Munfordville and at Perryville, Kentucky. They first served in a brigade commanded by Brigadier General Trapier. From December 1862, the brigade was commanded by Colonel Arthur Manigault and was known as "Manigault's Brigade."

In June of 1862, Beauregard was called back east and command of the Army of Mississippi was given to General Braxton Bragg. Battle flags for this command were purchased through contract with a New Orleans sailmaker named Cassidy. Using a Washington (Louisiana) Artillery flag as his inspiration, he created a battle flag that was distinctively different from its eastern cousin. The first examples were square, but the subsequent issues were rectangular, made of bunting with a wide pink border. There were twelve six-pointed stars on the St. Andrew's cross. A narrow white bunting border on the hoist had nine whipped eyelets for attachment to the staff. One example is 42½" (hoist) x 73½" (fly).

In the possession of a private collector.

10th Regiment Infantry
South Carolina Volunteers

The **10th Regiment Infantry** was organized on May 31, 1861, the last of ten regiments authorized by the State Act of December 17, 1860. Its first commander was Colonel Arthur M. Manigault. Throughout the history of the regiment, they remained with their original commander, first in Manigault's Brigade, Army of Mississippi (April-November, 1862), then in Manigault's Brigade, Army of Tennessee (November 1862 - April 1865), with whom they surrendered in North Carolina on April 26, 1865.

They saw action at Corinth, Murfreesboro, Chickamauga, Chattanooga, Atlanta, Franklin, Nashville, and Bentonville.

This flag of the 10th S.C. Regiment is a standard Army of Tennessee 1864 pattern battle flag. It is constructed of red and blue bunting with white cotton fimbriation and edging. It was issued in the spring of 1864, possibly to replace their Army of Mississippi 1862 pattern battle flag, which would have been issued to the regiment upon its arrival in Corinth.

This flag was saved from capture in a rather remarkable way during the Carolina campaign. This adventure was related by Sgt. Albert Myers at the flag's presentation to the state in 1925. *(See the following excerpt from* The State, *February 5, 1925)*

South Carolina Confederate Relic Room & Museum, Columbia, S.C.

WAR TORN FLAGS GIVEN TO STATE

Colors of Two Regiments in Relic Room

CEREMONY AT NOON

General Irvine Walker and James C. Sullivan Make Addresses

War torn and tattered, the battle flags of the Third and Tenth South Carolina regiments, Confederate States of America - enhaloed by the valor of South Carolinians and consecrated in their blood - were given yesterday into the keeping of the state of South Carolina.

Two torn bits of bunting, crossed with stars and bars, under which men marched out half a century and more agone to death.

"Once ten thousands hailed it gladly, And ten thousands wildly, madly, Swore it should forever wave."

Yesterday only a little group, weary and some of them near to that inevitable crossing of the river.

Some of them in tears, these veterans of a "fallen cause" and a "conquered banner" watched and listened with members of the two houses, Daughters of the Confederacy and others to the solemn ceremonies of presentation at noon in the hall of the house of representatives. Once the silence was broken by the old "rebel yell." And so the end.

The flag of the tenth regiment-recruited from the former districts of Horry, Marion, Williamsburg, Georgetown and Charleston - was presented by Gen. C. Irvine Walker of Charleston in whose possession it had been since the sur-render; the flag of the Third regiment - composed of four companies from Newberry, four from Laurens and two from Spartanburg county - was presented by Representative James A. Sullivan of Laurens, speaking in behalf of O.G. Thompson of Laurens, one of the few survivors of that command.

Briefly the histories of the two regiments were told by General Walker and by Mr. Sullivan - reading a paper prepared by Mr. Thompson. Albert A. Myers, the last color bearer of the Tenth, was heard in an account of an adventure with the regimental colors at the battle of Bentonville and then Gov. Thomas McLeod in the name of the state made the address of acceptance, receiving the two banners, he said, that forever they might recall to sons and aliens alike "what a glorious history is our heritage." By the governor the flags were given to Mrs. C.H. Girardeau, assistant curator of the state relic room, and Mrs. John C. Coulter, president of the Wade Hampton chapter, Daughters of the Confederacy, who carried them from the hall to the places prepared for them in the relic room. Gen. W.A. Clark, commanding the South Carolina division, United Confederate veterans, presided at the ceremonies.

Flag of Tenth

The flag of the Tenth regiment was first brought into the hall, carried by Senator D.A. Spivey of Horry, and escorted by a guard of honor: General Clark, the veterans of Camp Hampton and the soldiers' home, presidents of the Columbia, Georgetown, Florence and Newberry chapters of the United Daughters of the Confederacy, descendants of the two regiments, among them 14 year old Robert B. McNulty, representing his grandfather, W.E. McNulty; Color Sergeant Albert A. Myers, J. Fraser Lyon; Governor McLeod and General Walker.

"I appreciate most highly the honor you have bestowed upon the old battle flag of my regiment in calling this joint session to allow me to present it, with all its treasured memories, to the state." General Walker said, "I thus thank you in the name of the glorious men, whose bravery and devotion clothed this old piece of rag with immortal glory."

"The Tenth South Carolina regiment was formed of companies from the old time districts of Horry, Marion, Williamsburg, Georgetown and Charleston. I entered the regiment as its adjutant, receiving the appointment because I had been adjutant at the Citadel. I was subsequently adjutant general of Manigault's brigade, of which the Tenth South Carolina regiment was a part and finally was sent back to the regiment as its lieutenant colonel. Colonel Pressley having been so desperately wounded July 22 in front of Atlanta, that he never could return to duty, the command of the regiment was thrown upon me except when I was absent on account of wounds.

The regiment was with the Nineteenth was a part, and finally was sent to the Western army, which it joined just after the battle of Shiloh. It remained with that army until the end. These regiments were placed in the same brigade and both, being largely reduced in numbers from active service, were during the Chickamauga campaign consol-idated. The battle flag of the senior regiment was used as the battle flag of the consolidated command.

Back to Our State

"In the winter of 1864-1865 what was left of the army was sent to South Carolina to confront Sherman. The army retired in front of the Federal advance and after reaching Charlotte was sent and took part in the battle of Kinston. I was wounded and was not with the regiment at the battle of Bentonville . . .I got back just in time to surrender my command. I inquired as to the flag of the Tenth South Carolina, asking why it was not being used as the colors of the consolidated command as before. I could get no information . . .As we started to march home, Capt. R.Z. Harllee handed me a package, with the distinct understanding that I was not to open it until I reached home. When I opened it I found this dear old flag. It was never surrendered.

"So much for the history of the flag.

"Pardon me if I now partially digress . . ."

And he turned aside from memories of the flag and regiment to propose that the state publish a history of the role of South Carolina and South Carolinians in the Confederate war.

"Governor," he resumed, "this precious relic of an immortal past I now turn over to you, representing as you so worthily do, the state of South Carolina. Let the state ever preserve it, as a memento of the 71,000 of her sons, who when the war tocsin sounded, valiantly sprang to arms to defend her, but more especially the 1,276 men of the Tenth South Carolina regiment who offered their lives and to the 461 of them who with matchless heroism died gloriously for the grand old state of South Carolina.

Not in Disgrace

The men who so gloriously supported it, were all South Carolinians, who in spite of every danger, scantily clad, many bare-footed, poorly fed and suffering the privations of the damned, with godlike heroism, stood by it, until the starry banners of the South were forever furled - not in disgrace - not in dishonor - but in immortal glory. Let her people, let the whole world know that these men were true to their principles, faithful to their state and battled bravely that our people should enjoy the constitutional liberty guaranteed by the constitution of the United States. Let it ever be a stimulus to her sons, inspiring them to equal devotion to their state and then it will not have floated in vain, nor those who gave their lives in its defense have died in vain.

"Take it Governor - it has been my love for 60 years. I can not do better, as my life's journey is nearly ended, than to entrust it to my state, which I have ever loved and served, and for which I offered my life.

Tenderly he clasped it to his breast for one more time and then surrendered it to the governor.

Color Sergeant Myers was then introduced to tell how at the battle of Bentonville, a day or two before General Lee surrendered, he and eight comrades had broken through the Federal lines with the flag, there to find themselves cut off and lost. A Yankee ordnance sergeant was captured "with his mule, bridle and saddle" and from him it was learned that they were behind Federal lines. For fear of capture the flag was torn from its staff and Sergeant Myers wrapped it around his body. Until night the little group lay hidden in the woods and then under cover of darkness the Confederates made their way around the line of battle, occasionally as the opportunity offered capturing some Federals. "We reached our lines the next morning, bringing in ourselves, 17 prisoners, the mule, bridle and saddle and this flag!"

The State, February 5, 1925

10th South Carolina, a painting by artist Rick Reeves, shows the wear pattern that is now visible on the flag in the Confederate Relic Room in Columbia.

11ᵗʰ Regiment Infantry
South Carolina Volunteers

The flag of the **11ᵗʰ S.C. Regiment,** purchased by the Quartermaster Department from *Hayden and Whilden* of Charleston on a bill dated February 10, 1863, was a 1ˢᵗ National pattern with the unit designation "11ᵗʰ Regt. S.C.V.," with each letter and numeral sewn to the white horizontal bar.

The 9ᵗʰ Infantry regiment was organized in the spring of 1861 and disbanded in April 1862 after its failed attempt to organize. It was reorganized on May 3, 1862, as the 11th Regiment, South Carolina Volunteers.

As part of Hagood's Brigade, the 11ᵗʰ Regiment saw action at Coosawhatchie (Pocotaligo) and Charleston harbor. The action at Pocotaligo was intense. Casualty returns from one company alone show one killed, nine wounded. The regiment went to Virginia with Hagood's Brigade and saw action at Drewry's Bluff, Cold Harbor, Petersburg, Weldon Railroad, and Fort Harrison.

The regiment participated in the Battle of Bentonville and was surrendered with the Army of Tennessee at Durham, N.C. on April 26, 1865.

In a private collection in Pennsylvania

11ᵗʰ Regiment Infantry
South Carolina Volunteers

The flag of the **11ᵗʰ S.C. Regiment** (War Dept. capture No. 530) was returned to the State of South Carolina by the U.S. War Department on March 25, 1905. There has been a little discussion concerning its place and date of capture. The confusion of battle at Weldon Railroad led to the filing of an erroneous report concerning the capture of flags. All evidence indicates that this flag was captured on February 20, 1865, at Town Creek Bridge, N.C., by Corporal Oliver Hughes, Company C, 12th Kentucky (U.S.).

This flag is 44³/₄" (hoist) x 45¹/₂" (fly, including a 2¹/₂" unbleached linen sleeve). The red field, blue cross, and white edging are of bunting. The thirteen stars are cotton and are 4¹/₂" wide. The battle honors are painted in black enamel in 1¹/₂" and ¹/₂" Roman uncials. WELDON R. ROAD is in 1¹/₂" block italics.

The condition of the fly edge, especially the corners, is torn and tattered, evidencing prolonged service. The two battle honors in the fly quadrant are barely legible.

In 1976, the flag was sold by the *King Street Antique Shop* of Charleston to Mr. James Brady. The flag's history between 1905 and 1976 is not known.

The flag of the 11th Regiment was momentarily the center of attention at the Battle of Weldon Rail Road, Virginia, on August 21, 1864. General Hagood's troops, the 11th Regiment included, struck a part of the Union line where the troops were in echelon and found themselves almost surrounded. Assuming that the Confederates would surrender, Union troops left their position to begin rounding up their now surrounded attackers. A Union captain, provost-marshal of the 4th Division, galloped out of a salley port, seized the colors of the 11th Regiment, and called upon them to surrender. At this point General Hagood arrived.

"Observing this, I made my way to them from the part of the line upon which I was, calling to the men to shoot him. They either did not hear me or were bewildered by the surrender of part of their number and failed to do so. When I got up to him I demanded the colors from him, and that he should go back into his own works, telling him he was

free to do so. He commenced arguing with me, upon our desperate position, and I cut him short, demanding a categorical reply. He said no, and I shot him from his horse. Giving the colors to my orderly and mounting his horse, I succeeded in withdrawing the men with as little loss as could have been expected from the terrible fire to which we were exposed."

After the fall of Petersburg and Richmond, the 11th Regiment returned to the Carolinas, and participated in the Fort Fisher campaign. These colors were captured on February 20, 1865. The 11th Regiment was surrendered with the Army of Tennessee at Durham, N.C. on April 26, 1865.

In the possession of a private collector.

12ᵗʰ Regiment Infantry
South Carolina Volunteers

Although this flag is not regular infantry size (it is actually closer to the 3' x 3' of an artillery flag), it is documented as the flag brought home by the regiment after the surrender. The following note is displayed with the flag at the South Carolina Relic Room and Museum.

"On October 30, 1907, this flag was presented to the State of South Carolina by Captain Allen Jones, a member of the regiment whose father, Colonel Cadwallader Jones, commanded the regiment. This flag was received by Governor Martin F. Ansel.

This flag was brought back to Rock Hill by Enoch Blackman after the surrender and held by him until about 1882, when an association of the regiment was formed and the flag donated to it. The flag was passed from one officer to another until Sgt. David Moore gave it to the state for safekeeping."

The 12ᵗʰ Regiment served under Brigadier Generals Maxcy Gregg and Samuel McGowan.

South Carolina Confederate Relic Room & Museum, Columbia, S.C.

13ᵗʰ Regiment Infantry
South Carolina Volunteers

For some time this flag was believed to be that of the 14ᵗʰ S.C. Regiment. However, modern work done by the Museum of the Confederacy, comparing notes from the National Archives Register of Captured Flags with independent research, identifies this flag as that of the 13*th* Regiment S.C. Infantry. The museum records show that it was "captured or surrendered during the Appomattox Campaign, April 1865."

The battle honors are painted in uppercase, white block letters, but are extremely faded and nearly illegible. Outer honors are 2" high, while the inner honors are 1³/₄" high. The diameter of the inner circle is 25". There are two honors on the reverse: CHANCELLORSVILLE along the hoist edge and FREDERICKSBURG along the upper edge.

The flag is listed as War Department Capture No. 431.

Museum of the Confederacy, Richmond, Va.

Brockman Guards

Company B, 13th Regiment Infantry, South Carolina Volunteers

Two brothers from Greenville District, S.C., were responsible for the raising of a company of infantry in the summer of 1861. For their efforts, Benjamin T. Brockman and Jesse K. Brockman were made respectively captain and first lieutenant of the company that bore their names. The **Brockman Guards** were mustered into Confederate service as Company B, 13th Regiment Infantry, South Carolina Volunteers. When the regimental commander, Colonel O.E. Edwards, was mortally wounded at Chancellorsville, Benjamin Brockman was made colonel of the 13th Regiment. At the terrible battle of Spottsylvania, on May 12, 1864, Colonel Brockman and his brother Jesse, at that time captain of the company, were both mortally wounded.

The flag of the Brockman Guards is constructed of blue silk. It is 37" (hoist) x 42" (fly), with 2" gold fringe on three sides. The reverse design shows the company name, BROCKMAN GUARDS, painted in gold block letters along a flowing line. Surrounding the name are eleven painted gold stars arranged in a circle, each pointing outward from the circle's center. This pattern is similar to a flag in the collection of the Charleston Museum, that of the South Carolina Rangers.

The obverse of the Brockman Guards flag is a seal showing a palmetto tree on the shore, a common design for early war company flags. The seal has deteriorated badly and is faded and cracked.

South Carolina Relic Room & Museum, Columbia, S.C.

14ᵗʰ Regiment Infantry
South Carolina Volunteers
The Hiding of the Colors

The following letter is recorded in John A. Chapman's *History of Edgefield County, South Carolina*. The original was published in the *Charleston News and Courier* on July 30, 1891. It was written by Rufus Harling of Clark's Hill, S.C. Harling was a private in Company K, 14ᵗʰ Regiment, and was wounded at Gettysburg and at the Wilderness. This letter tells of a poignant moment in the last days of the war when a small band of South Carolina infantrymen, being pursued by a tenacious host of Union cavalry, realized that hope was lost. Their thoughts and concerns turned to their flag.

"In the early days of 1865 McGowan's Brigade was holding the right wing of General Lee's army. Early in the morning we were ordered to move out of our works, by the right flank, in the direction of the South Side Railroad, to cover the retreating and shattered forces of Lee's army, and soon after we had gotten on the march Captain Dunlap's Battalion of sharpshooters was ordered to the rear, deployed, and ordered to fall back in rear of the brigade. Soon after crossing a small stream we heard the roaring as that of distant thunder, which we soon discovered to be the mighty host of Sheridan's Cavalry in hot pursuit, and each cavalryman seemed to have a man behind him. As soon as they would come within range, the men behind would dismount and fire on us. We would return the fire as often as possible. Thus for some distance we were hotly pursued.

"As soon as the brigade reached the South Side Railroad it halted, and formed a line of battle. Hastily piling up some rails as a protection from the advancing foe, which was a welcome cover to the hard pressed sharp-shooters, we fell in with the brigade as we found it, but not long to rest, for soon the enemy emerged from the woods into the open field in a splendid line of infantry to charge a little remnant of men. As they advanced across an open field they were allowed to come within easy range of our rifles. It then seemed that every man was determined to make his shots count, for after two or three volleys the enemy fell back in disorder to the woods from where they came. Receiving reinforcements, rapidly formed and moved to our left, and with their overwhelming forces we were compelled to retreat in disorder.

"After crossing the railroad in the direction of the Appomattox River, I came up with the Color-Bearer of the Fourteenth South Carolina Regiment, and around him were about twenty-five men of the First, Twelfth, Thirteenth, and Fourteenth Regiments. Not having time to consult as to the better way of safety, we moved hastily on to the Appomattox River, thinking we might cross and join Longstreet's Corps, which was thought to be retreating up the river from Richmond. Finding the river considerably swollen and no way of crossing, we made our way up the river as best we could. Night coming on, we lay our wornout selves down to sleep, and a glorious sleep it was, such as we had not had in several nights. Next morning we were up early, ate a scanty breakfast, and continued to

move up the river, thinking perhaps we might find some way of escape. On reaching a hill we found the enemy had gotten ahead of us, and that we must soon be made prisoners. We then collected around the Color-Bearer, and determined to conceal the colors of the Fourteenth South Carolina Regiment. Then I, assisted by two others, raised a large flat rock, under which our Color-Bearer placed the colors of the Fourteenth Regiment.

"Captain W.L. Delph, now of Augusta, Ga., recently informed me that a gentleman by the name of Bunch, from the lower part of this State, was sent back to Virginia after the colors of the First South Carolina Regiment, which were placed with the colors of the Fourteenth South Carolina Regiment, under the same rock, and that Bunch also got the colors of the Fourteenth Regiment. If so, where are they? Any information respecting them will be thankfully received."

> *RUFUS HARLING*
> *Clark's Hill, S.C.*

This letter continues a mystery. In the spring of 1863, the regiments of McGowan's Brigade were issued a 3rd Bunting Issue battle flag. Peculiar about these flags was the method of regimental identification. Above the center star was stenciled the regimental number in gold. Below the star was stenciled the regiment's state, also in gold. It appears that none of these S.C. flags have survived the war. Surviving examples of this issue, notably the 1st and 14th Tennessee, have battle honors painted in blue block letters, all in horizontal lettering, in all four red quadrants.

Even in 1891, Harling's attention to detail reflects a keen memory of these events. The hiding of the flag under a stone must be true. If Mr. "Bunch" actually did retrieve the flags, there is no record of it, and the flag of the 14th Regiment, as well as those of the 1st, 12th, and 13th, is still missing.

14ᵗʰ Regiment Infantry
South Carolina Volunteers

Although this flag is not known to be the Regimental flag of the **14ᵗʰ S.C. Infantry Regiment,** it has documented ties to that regiment. Billy Covar, color bearer, brought this rectangular, hand-made battle flag home to Edgefield County for the 14ᵗʰ Regiment. It is cared for by the United Daughters of the Confederacy and is on display at the Red Shirt Shrine in Edgefield, S.C.

It is 34" (hoist) x 48" (fly) and has gold fringe on three sides. The blue silk St. Andrew's cross is composed of one bar laid over another and sewn to the red silk field. Each blue bar is 4³/₈" wide. There are thirteen 4³/₈" diameter stars sewn to the cross. The spacing of the stars varies from 6⁷/₈" to 9¹/₈".

The white fimbriation is odd in that it is piping instead of ribbon.

This flag is in a very deteriorated state. There is much damage done to the obverse by the effects of age, and there is deterioration along the fold lines.

Oakley Park Red Shirt Shrine, Edgefield, S.C.

Ryan Guards

Co. H, 14th Regiment Infantry, South Carolina Volunteers

 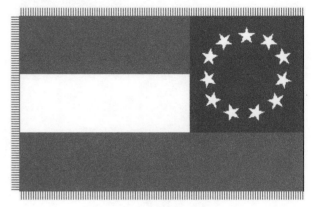

The flag of the Ryan Guards is 27" (hoist) x 44" (fly). The obverse is blue with a white border surrounded on three sides by gold fringe. The palmetto tree, crescent, and letters are white cotton. The reverse is a standard 1st National with eleven stars.

South Carolina Confederate Relic Room & Museum, Columbia, S.C.

McCalla Rifles

Co. I, 14th Regiment Infantry, South Carolina Volunteers

The flag of the **McCalla Rifles** is in very fragile condition. The white silk has discolored to a buff hue and the red is now reddish-orange. The flag is 37" (hoist) x 41" (fly), with silver fringe on three sides. The silk star is badly shredded with many vertical splits.

South Carolina State Museum, Columbia, S.C.

15ᵗʰ Regiment Infantry
South Carolina Volunteers

Eleven of the original thirteen stars remain on this battle flag of the **15ᵗʰ S.C. Regiment.** The bottom part of the lower red quarter panel is gone. The honors are in uppercase, stylized Gothic letters and are applied in white paint on the obverse side only. The outer honors are 2"-high letters. The inner honors are in 1¾"-high letters. The honor FREDERICKSBURG is believed to have once been in the missing bottom portion of the lower quarter panel. All of the battle honors are very faint, the upper and lower honors being barely visible.

Much of the fly edge is missing, including the top right star and bottom right star. No battle honors are visible in what remains of the fly quadrant.

The red field and blue cross are of wool. The fimbriation and stars are of cotton. The border is of wool and the hoist is of canvas with three whipped eyelets.

The battle flag of the 15ᵗʰ Regiment was captured at Cedar Creek, Virginia, on October 19, 1864, by W.A. Hough of Company E, 8ᵗʰ Indiana Volunteers.

Museum of the Confederacy, Richmond, Va.

Lexington Guards
Co. C, 15ᵗʰ Regiment Infantry, South Carolina Volunteers

The **Lexington Guards** were organized by Capt. F.L. Lewie in Lexington District and were accepted as part of the quota called by South Carolina on July 15, 1861. The company served in the 15th Regiment, S.C.V. They fought at Hilton Head/Port Royal on Nov. 7, 1861, and at Secessionville on June 16, 1862. Later they were transferred to Virginia. They served under several commanders, but are most often associated with Kershaw's Brigade. Their last battle was at Bentonville, N.C., March 19-21, 1865.

The white silk flag shown above is 28" (hoist) x 37" (fly) and is bordered on three sides with 2" gold fringe. The hand-painted palmetto tree is 22½" tall. The fronds measure 10½" wide and the base is 23" wide. Eleven 2"-diameter gold stars, bronze shaded, arch above the palmetto. An interesting detail is the depiction of seven tiny palmettos at the base of the larger, the symbolism of course being that from the first state to secede came a Confederation of seven states.

Both flags are at the South Carolina Confederate Relic Room & Museum, Columbia, S.C.

Martin Guards
Co. A, 13th Regiment Infantry, S.C.V.

This strikingly similar flag is 40" x 47". Arched above the palmetto is ANIMIS OPIBUSQUE PARATI. In a reverse arch below the palmetto is PRESENTED BY THE LADIES OF LAURENS.

16ᵗʰ Regiment Infantry
South Carolina Volunteers

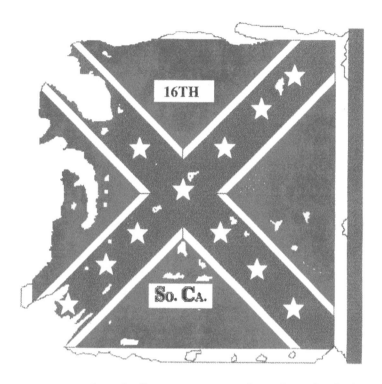

This Charleston Depot battle flag was issued to the 16ᵗʰ S.C. Regiment before they left by train for the west. Sent in May 1863 as part of a brigade commanded by Brigadier General States Rights Gist, they served throughout the war in the Army of Tennessee, and returned at last to the east to take part in the Carolina campaign. They surrendered with General Johnston in North Carolina.

This flag is identified with unit patches. Centered on the upper red quadrant is a 3¼" x 8½" cotton patch on which is printed, in 2"-high black Roman uncial figures, "16TH." Centered on the lower quadrant is a 3¾" x 8¼" patch, on which is printed in highly stylized, outlined, and shaded 2½" block letters, "SO. CA."

Major B.B. Smith brought both the flags of the 16ᵗʰ and the 24ᵗʰ Regiments home to South Carolina after the war.

South Carolina Confederate Relic Room & Museum, Columbia, S.C.

Sharpsburg Flag

This 52½" x 56" battle flag is made of red, blue, and yellow wool, with white cotton trim. The blue wool St. Andrew's cross is bordered with white cotton fimbriation and has thirteen white cotton stars. Three outside edges of the flag have 1½" yellow wool borders. The hoist is a 2¼" heavy white cotton band with loops for attaching to the staff.

This flag, War Department capture No. 31, was captured at the battle of Sharpsburg, Maryland, on September 17, 1862, by Pvt. Thomas Hare, Co. D, 89th N.Y. Infantry.

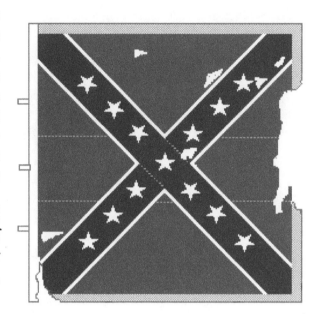

Charleston Museum, Charleston, S.C.

South Carolina Troops at the Battle of Sharpsburg

Kershaw's Brigade	Evans' Brigade	Gregg's Brigade
2nd S.C. Regt.	Holcombe's Legion	Orr's Rifles
3rd S.C. Regt.	17th S.C. Regt.	1st S.C. Regt.
7th S.C. Regt.	18th S.C. Regt.	12th S.C. Regt.
8th S.C. Regt.	22nd S.C. Regt.	13th S.C. Regt.
23rd S.C. Regt.	14th S.C. Regt.	
Jenkins' Brigade	Drayton's Brigade	Wofford's Brigade
1st (Hagood's) S.C. Regt.	15th S.C. Regt.	Hampton's Legion
2nd Rifles		
5th S.C. Regt.		
6th S.C. Regt.		

Hagood's Brigade
South Carolina Volunteers

This flag fragment is approximately 8" x 36" in size. The painted upright block letters are 4½" high. The overall length of the word HAGOOD'S is 33½".

On March 7, 1882, a former South Carolina Confederate, Mr. C. P. A. Brown, wrote a letter to then-governor Johnson Hagood reminiscing about the last days of the war. He presented the governor with this fragment, dramatically describing the "woeful day at High Point, after the battle of Bentonville, when our portion of the army surrendered."

When the time came to turn over the battle flags, a number of men of the brigade tore their flag into pieces, each preserving a portion, rather than surrender it. Brown mistakenly referred to this flag as, "a part of the same flag that you rescued from the Yankee Col., who you shot when demanding your surrender, and brought out safely with your clothes riddled with bullets . . ." [reference to an incident at Weldon Railroad.] The letter was signed "C. P. A. Brown, Co'y B, 7th S.C. Battallion."

Brown made many mistakes in his letter, but his intention was good. Governor Hagood conveyed his thanks to Brown, recognizing the fragment as "a part of the Head Quarters Flag of the Brigade. It was used to indicate HeadQuarters when we were encamped or bivouacked."

Hagood graciously corrected Brown, saying the flag to which the former soldier referred was actually the flag of the 11th Regiment, admitting that he himself had gotten it confused with another flag at the time.

Special Collections, Emory University, Atlanta, Ga.

One other fragment of this flag is known to the author; a star in the Confederate Museum. There probably are more in existence.

It is likely that the Brigade flag was of a 1st National pattern and may have resembled the illustration at the right.

Hagood's Brigade
South Carolina Volunteers

> This flag fragment of a 6"-diameter star sewn to a blue swatch is a remnant of Hagood's Brigade flag, torn to shreds at the surrender of the Army. The size of the star would indicate an overall flag size of larger than 3' x 5'. The grain of the cloth and angle of the star would place the star either in the top right or bottom left of the circle on a 1st National pattern.

It's easy to overlook fragments such as the one above. It certainly doesn't look like a flag. But much can be determined even from such an insignificant artifact. The angle of the star relative to the grain of the fabric seems to be a clue that the parent flag was a 1st National. Even if one rotates the swatch, the star still seems to be in a most likely position of one o'clock on the canton. The member units in Hagood's brigade were issued 1st Nationals. It would seem appropriate for the brigade to maintain one.

Flags seem "balanced" when certain ratios are maintained. One of these balancing ratios is the width of the star to the width of the canton. In a seven-star 1st National, such as the Fort Sumter flag, the most attractive ratio is around 1:5. For an eleven-star flag, the ratio is closer to 1:6. Using these ratios, an overall picture of a flag can be determined even from such a small fragment.

The above star's width of 6" would signify a canton approximately 36" square. Using the specified pattern for the 1st National flag, a canton this size would make the overall flag 4½' feet by 7', an appropriate size for a staff or garrison flag.

It is most likely that the preceding fragment upon which is written HAGOOD'S is part of the same flag as this star.

Confederate Museum, Charleston, S.C.

21ˢᵗ Regiment Infantry
South Carolina Volunteers

This 36" x 60" flag was made for the 21ˢᵗ **South Carolina Regiment** by Hayden & Whilden of Charleston, South Carolina, on February 10, 1863. It is made of wool. The cloth letters are individually handsewn to the center bar.

The 21ˢᵗ Regiment saw action on Morris Island on July 10, 1863, during the Federals' initial assault on the southern end of the island and during the first assault on Battery Wagner the following morning. During this action the regiment lost its battle flag. The above flag flew over their camp on Morris Island. Battery Wagner was abandoned in September, 1863. The regiment was transferred to Virginia, arriving on May 6, 1864, in time to fight against Butler's Army of the James. They surrendered at Greensboro, N.C., on April 26, 1865.

In June 1998, the flag of the *21ˢᵗ Regiment, South Carolina Volunteers* was offered for sale by antique dealer Gary Hendershott. At that time it was in a private collection.

21st Regiment Infantry
South Carolina Volunteers

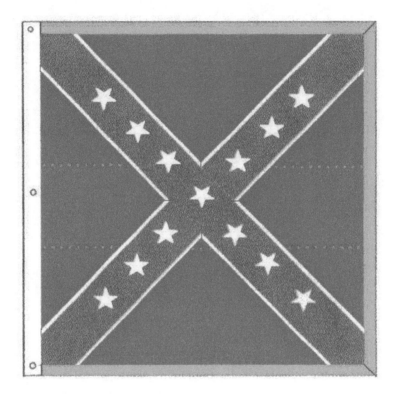

This flag of the **21st Regiment S.C. Infantry** is of wool bunting, with small cotton stars more gathered to the center than evenly spaced, and with an orange border. Because the flag was captured so soon after its manufacture, the orange border is unfaded and still retains its original color. Many flags of this issue have borders that have faded to yellow or tan. This flag has a white canvas hoist with three evenly spaced eyelets.

On July 10, 1863, in the first Union assault on Battery Wagner, the assaulting brigade overran the Confederate rifle pits on Morris Island. The 9th Regiment Maine Infantry captured the battle flag of the 21st S.C. Infantry. It was returned to the governor of South Carolina by the governor of Maine in 1927. (See *Confederate Veteran*, Vol. XXXVI, No. 3: March 1928, p. 104, "Flags Returned to the South.")

South Carolina Confederate Relic Room & Museum, Columbia, S.C.

21st Regiment Infantry
South Carolina Volunteers

The battle flag of the 21st South Carolina Regiment Infantry was captured at Weldon Railroad, Virginia, on August 21, 1864, along with two other unmarked flags of Hagood's Brigade. There is an equal chance that the above flag, War Dept. capture No. 155, could be that of the 25th Regiment. (See the entries regarding the 7th Battalion and the 25th Regiment.)

The above flag is 46" (hoist) x 48¾" (fly) and is made of red and blue wool. The 4"-diameter stars spaced at 8" intervals help to identify this flag as a Charleston Depot issue flag, disbursed to the regiment before they left South Carolina. It is hand sewn of quadrant construction. The stars have folded hems. The hoist edge is a 2½" sleeve made of blue wool.

Museum of the Confederacy, Richmond, Virginia

Wallace's Brigade
South Carolina Volunteers

This famous brigade of South Carolinians was first led by General Nathan Evans, then by General Stephen Elliott, and lastly by General William Wallace. Often called the "Tramp Brigade" for their many hard marches, they served the Confederacy in the entire triangle formed by Mississippi, Florida, and Virginia

The Brigade was composed of the Seventeenth, Eighteenth, Twenty-second, and Twenty-third Regiments, and the Holcombe Legion. In 1864, the Twenty-sixth Regiment was added to the Brigade.

After all their hard marches, they found themselves in Virginia in the spring of 1865, marching for their lives, pursued by Sheridan's Federal cavalry. On April 1, 1865, they were engaged by Sheridan, beginning the battle of Five Forks. G.W. Coleman, of the 17th Regt., remembered that, "we soon began to exchange shots. This was kept up for some time. Finally, on looking back, we saw a dense column of yanks in our rear . . . We were firing some at the rear and some in front . . . They came rushing on, in front and rear and soon had us prisoners."

The above flag, War Department Capture No. 279, was captured at Five Forks by Corporal August Kause, Company H, 15th N.Y. Heavy Artillery (serving as infantry).

Museum of the Confederacy, Richmond, Va.

24ᵗʰ Regiment Infantry
South Carolina Volunteers

On April 15, 1862, the 24ᵗʰ S.C. Regiment became the first regiment to enlist for the duration of the war, and suffered its first fatalities that summer at the battle of Secessionville, S.C.

The regiment left Charleston in May of 1863 in response to General Pemberton's pleas for reinforcements at Vicksburg, Mississippi. They were attached to the Army of Tennessee. They were engaged in the defense of Jackson, Mississippi, and later fought at Chattanooga, Dalton, Kennesaw Mountain, Atlanta, Franklin, and Nashville.

On the road to Nashville, a small number of men from Company I, 24ᵗʰ Regiment, with their lieutenant Jim Tillman, held a pass, severely delaying the passage of the Union army. The color bearer, Adam Carpenter, placed this flag on the works. It was cut down three times by enemy fire, only to be raised again. Finally, with the butt of the flagstaff in his hand, Carpenter waved the flag in defiance of the Union forces. After the battle of Nashville, the 24ᵗʰ Regiment returned east and participated in the Carolinas campaign, finally laying down their arms at Durham, N.C., on April 26, 1865.

The unsurrendered flag of the 24ᵗʰ Regiment was brought home by Major B.B. Smith.

25th Regiment Infantry
South Carolina Volunteers

This Charleston Depot flag of the 24th Regiment Infantry has been heavily damaged over the years by field use and souvenir seekers. Many stars and sections of flag are missing.

The flag is 44" (hoist) x 47" (fly). Centered in the top quadrant is a 3¼" x 6¾" cotton patch, on which is printed in 2"-high black Roman uncial letters **24TH**. Although it is now missing, a victim of souvenir gatherers, in the lower quadrant was a patch, roughly 3" x 8", on which was printed in highly stylized, outlined and shaded block letters, SO.CA. These types of patches were common on many Charleston Depot flags.

South Carolina Confederate Relic Room & Museum, Columbia, S.C.

The 11th Battalion Infantry (Eutaw Battalion) was organized on February 24, 1862, under the command of Major Charles H. Simonton. They saw action on June 16, 1862, at Secessionville. The increase of the battalion led to the formation of the **25th Regiment Infantry** (Eutaw Regiment) on July 22, 1862. Simonton was promoted to colonel and commanded the regiment. In the late summer of that year, they were attached to General Johnson Hagood's brigade, with whom they served until they were surrendered at Durham Station, N.C. on April 26, 1865.

They took part in battles in South Carolina at Jones Island, Grimball's Landing, and Charleston Harbor. They fought in Virginia at Port Walthall Junction, Swift Creek, Drewry's Bluff, Cold Harbor, Petersburg, Weldon

Railroad, and Fort Harrison. They took part in the defense of Fort Fisher, N.C., on January 13-15, 1865, participated in the Carolinas Campaign, and fought their last battle at Bentonville, N.C. on March 19-21, 1865.

Washington Light Infantry, Charleston, S.C.

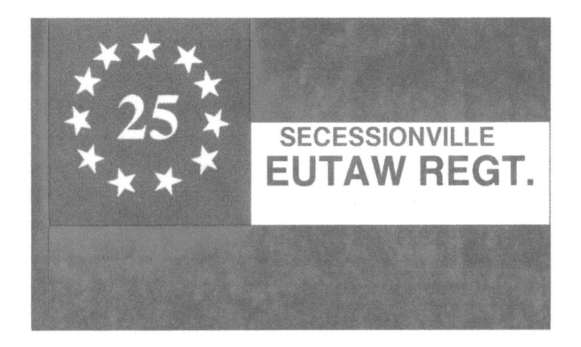

25th Regiment Infantry
South Carolina Volunteers

This flag is listed in one photographic essay of artifacts as being that of the **25th Regiment Infantry,** South Carolina Volunteers. It could also be the flag of the 21st Regiment Infantry. There is actually a 50 percent chance that it is either. At Weldon Railroad, Virginia, on August 21, 1864, General Johnson Hagood's Brigade was engaged in a ferocious and hectic assault that led to the capture of three flags. The battle flags of the 7th Battalion, 21st Regiment, and 25th Regiment, South Carolina Volunteers, all unmarked, were captured that day. The flag with War Dept. Capture No. 154 has a red hoist and may be that of the 7th Battalion. (See article on 7th Battalion Infantry.)

The above flag, War Dept. Capture No. 156, is 45½" (hoist) x 48" (fly) and is made of red and blue wool. The dimensions of the stars (4¼") placed at 8" intervals on a 8"-wide cross identify this flag as Charleston Depot manufactory. It is handsewn.

The overall condition of this flag is listed as "good."

Museum of the Confederacy, Richmond, Virginia

26ᵗʰ Regiment Infantry
South Carolina Volunteers

The **26ᵗʰ South Carolina Regiment** was organized on September 9, 1862, by the consolidation of the 6ᵗʰ and 9ᵗʰ Infantry battalions. It served in Charleston, South Carolina, from 1862 until early 1863, when it was sent to Mississippi, where it was engaged in the siege of Jackson. Returning to Charleston in August, the regiment participated in the repulse of Union forces during the siege of August and September 1863. It served in South Carolina until the spring of 1864, when it was sent to Virginia to serve in General William Wallace's brigade.

South Carolina Confederate Relic Room & Museum, Columbia, S.C.

In the spring of 1864, the regiment carried this Charleston Depot battle flag into action at Bermuda Hundred and Petersburg, Virginia. At Fort Steadman, on March 25, 1865, the color bearer of the 26th Regiment, Samuel J. Reid, was knocked down by the explosion of a shell. Captain H. L. Buck retrieved the flag but was captured, along with many of his men.

The missing star was likely removed as a reward for the Union soldier credited with capturing the flag.

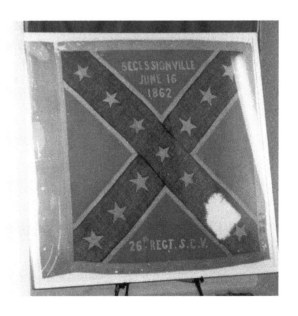

Charleston Light Infantry
South Carolina Volunteers

The **Charleston Light Infantry** served under Captain Thomas Y. Simons first in the 1ˢᵗ South Carolina Volunteer Infantry Battalion and later in the 27ᵗʰ Regiment Infantry. Organized in March 1862, this company was engaged at the battle of Secessionville on James Island in June of that year.

When General Pierre G.T. Beauregard took command of the Charleston area, he found that flags in this unusual design had been adopted by at least four local garrison regiments. This flag was patterned after a proposed national color that had been recommended by the *Charleston Mercury* in March 1862.

The flag is 23½" (hoist) x 28½" (fly) and is made of red and white wool sewn in four quadrants. The blue silk shield is 9½" high x 11½" wide and is appliqued both on the obverse and the reverse of the flag. SECESSIONVILLE is written in uppercase, block letters, 1¾" high. C.L.I is in uppercase, Roman letters, 2" high. There is gold metallic fringe, 1½" wide, now only on the top and bottom but which was probably on the fly end as well at one time.

Museum of the Confederacy, Richmond, Virginia.

27th Regiment Infantry
South Carolina Volunteers

The **27th S.C. Regiment** was organized by the consolidation of the 1st (Charleston) Infantry Battalion (later Companies A,B,C,D,H,I—27th Regt.) and the 1st Battalion S.C. Sharpshooters (later Companies E,F,G—27th Regt.). Prior to the organization of the regiment, its members in the parent battalions served at Secessionville, Fort Wagner, Fort Sumter, and Pocotaligo. After organization in late 1863, the regiment went to Virginia as part of General Johnson Hagood's Brigade. In Virginia they fought at Drewry's Bluff, Bermuda Hundred, Cold Harbor,

Petersburg, and Weldon Railroad, where the above flag was captured.

The following report by Union Brig. Gen. Charles Griffin explains in part the confusion of Weldon Railroad.

> "General Hagood's brigade struck a part of our line where the troops were in echelon and they found themselves almost surrounded, and every one thinking they had surrendered, ceased firing. Troops immediately advanced to bring them in when their officers commenced firing, and Captain Daily, provost-marshall of the Fourth Division was shot by general Hagood. In the mixed condition of our men and the enemy, our line could not fire, and many of the enemy escaped. On General Griffin's advance, F.C. Anderson, of the Eighteenth Massachusetts, captured the battle flag of the Twenty-seventh South Carolina." OR, XLII, pt. 1, p. 431

This Charleston Depot flag was returned to South Carolina by the U.S. War Department in 1905. For a time it was in private hands, but it is now back at the Relic Room.

South Carolina Confederate Relic Room & Museum, Columbia, S.C.

Calhoun Light Battery

1st Company (Co. A), Battalion of Artillery; Regular Army of S.C.

This unit was raised for twelve months' State service during January 1861. Officers were Capt. William R. Calhoun, 1st Lt. Thomas M. Wagner, 1st Lt. William C. Preston, and 2nd Lt. S. Seagreaves. The company was part of the garrison at Fort Moultrie on April 12, 1861. Along with four other companies, A-E, they were mustered into Confederate service in May 1861, as the 1st S.C. Artillery Battalion. Company A remained at that post until July 4, 1861, when it left Charleston with orders to proceed to Virginia to be "employed at the seat of the war as a corps of flying artillery." Company F was organized in October and Company G was organized in November 1861. Companies H and I were organized in February 1862, and the following month the Battalion was reorganized as the 1st Artillery Regiment.

During early September, Company A was attached to the 4th Regiment Infantry and was still on active service in Virginia on December 30, 1861.

By September 1862, W.R. Calhoun had received a promotion to colonel in the Regular Army of South Carolina and, on the fifth day of that month, was killed in a duel with Major Alfred Rhett at Charleston.

The 38⅝" (hoist) x 48⅞" (fly) flag is made of blue silk, with the reverse embroidered with a palmetto tree in chenille with a star of gold sequins above. The word READY is arched above the star; SOUTH CAROLINA is reverse-arched below the tree. Centered on the obverse is a crescent embroidered in gold-colored silk and sequins. CRESCIT ALBA is embroidered in an arch over the crescent, with CALHOUN ARTILLERY reverse-arched below. The banner is edged on three sides with gold metallic fringe.

The Charleston Museum, Charleston, S.C.

1st Regiment Artillery
South Carolina Volunteers

The flag of the **1st Regiment S.C. Artillery** is of blue-and-white silk. A Charleston newspaper editor suggested this distinctive design when the first national flag of the Confederacy (Stars and Bars) was confused in battle with the flag of the United States. (See *Carolina Light Infantry* and *3rd Cavalry Battalion*).

This flag was donated to the Charleston Museum by the City of Charleston. There are holes in it where tacks held it in a case at City Hall.

It is 56" (hoist) x 59½" (fly). There is gold fringe, 1¾" wide, along three sides. The center circle is painted in gold and red on cream silk. In the circle are a palmetto tree, the letters S.C., and crossed cannons. The top quadrant has a cartouche painted with MOULTRIE/AP^L 12th & 13th, 1861. The bottom quadrant has a similar cartouche with SUMTER/APRIL 7th, 1863.

It is in poor condition. The paint is flaking badly, especially on previous crease lines. The entire flag has been rebacked (white portions are replacements) and sandwiched between netting.

The Charleston Museum, Charleston, South Carolina

Inglis Light Artillery (Charles' Battery)
Company D, 2ⁿᵈ S.C. Regiment

The **Inglis Light Artillery** was the only light artillery battery in the 2ⁿᵈ Regiment. The other batteries were heavy artillery.

The Misses Helen and Constance Cary of Richmond, Virginia made this flag for the Charles Battery of Light Artillery while the company was stationed at James Island.

This battery saw action at Secessionville, Legareville, Cocked Hat, Church Flats, Honey Hill, and other minor engagements with gunboats along the Atlantic coast. The battery was held in reserve at Averysboro and Bentonville, North Carolina.

The flag is 34" square with a red bunting sleeve for attachment to the staff. The cross is made of 5⅛" bars bordered with ⅞"-1" fimbriation.

South Carolina Confederate Relic Room & Museum, Columbia, S.C.

3rd Regiment S.C. Regular Artillery
(Formerly 1st Regiment, S.C. Regular Infantry)

The ravages of war, time, and souvenir hunters have taken their toll on the flag of the **3rd S.C. Heavy Artillery.** This 46⅝" (hoist) by 46⅛" (fly) wool flag is in extremely poor condition. The lower right quarter is almost entirely gone. Three holes in the lower left arm of the St. Andrew's cross mark where stars have been removed. One hole in the upper left arm shows another star's removal. Only six stars remain on the blue cross. The museum card notes that the flag flew over Fort Sumter during the fort's third bombardment (July 7 - September 4, 1864), in which 14,666 shots were fired at the fort.

Thomas A. Huguenin presented this flag to the Sumter Guards, South Carolina Volunteers, in 1875. It was turned over to the Charleston Museum on December 27, 1941. Major Huguenin served in the 1st S.C. Regulars (3rd S.C. Volunteer Heavy Artillery) at Fort Sumter in 1864.

The Charleston Museum, Charleston, S.C.

Beaufort Volunteer Artillery

Elliott's/Stuart's (S.C.) Artillery Company

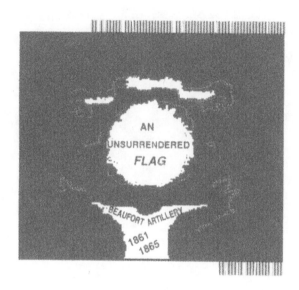

The **Beaufort Artillery Company** was founded in 1776, and served through the War for Independence. The company was on duty at the siege of Charleston and was included in the surrender of May 1780. During the early years of the nineteenth century, it maintained its position in the state's militia defenses, and trained with field pieces as well as heavy artillery.

At the Battle of Port Royal, November 7, 1861, this command, under Captain Stephen Elliott, Jr., was assigned to duty on the Bay Point side of the harbor. It was the only artillery garrison on that side, and was involved in fierce fighting.

Soon after the fall of Port Royal, this battery was equipped as a light battery, and served admirably in battles at *Pocotaligo,* on October 22, 1862, and *Honey Hill,* on November 30, 1864.

The flag is 33" (hoist) x 41" (fly) and has 3" fringe. It is only recognizable as the Beaufort Artillery Company flag because of a note attached to it in the Relic Room. The note says that the center (which surely was some form of State seal) was shot out by enemy cannon fire. This could well be true, since the Beaufort Battery was often in the heat of battle, doing duty in counter-battery fire.

South Carolina Confederate Relic Room & Museum, Columbia, S.C.

Chesterfield Artillery
Coit's Battery

The flag of the **Chesterfield Artillery** is 36" (hoist) x 41" (fly) and is made of two layers of blue silk. It is edged on three sides with 2" gold metallic fringe. It was made by a group of South Carolina ladies and presented to Captain Coit's Battery of Artillery. The flag is in extremely fragile condition, with much fabric shredding.

Museum of the Confederacy, Richmond, Va.

Centered on the obverse of the Chesterfield Artillery flag is a 15"-high palmetto rendered in gold paint. The crescent is also painted and is 7½" diameter. The Latin mottoes ANIMAS OPIBUSQUE PARTI and DUM SPIRO SPERO SPES are painted in gold block letters 2" high.

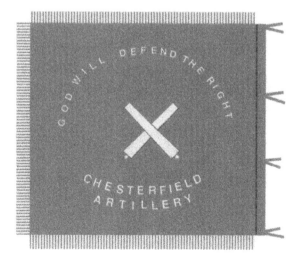

Centered on the reverse of the **Chesterfield Artillery** flag are crossed cannon barrels, each one 12" long and painted in gold with brown and yellow detail. Arched above the cannons is the motto, GOD WILL DEFEND THE RIGHT, in gold painted block letters, 3" high. The unit name is arched below the cannon in 3½" block letters.

Washington Artillery

Company A, Artillery Battalion, Hampton Legion

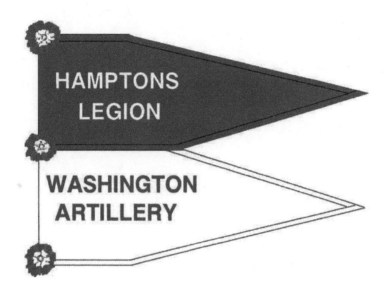

On June 11, 1861, J. Randolph Mordecai, whose daughter made this guidon, presented it to Captain Hart. In presenting the flag, Mr. Mordecai said:

"Its colors and symbols of our cause and our purpose, its simple white indicating the sacred truth of the one, the red telling you that in vindicating that truth, every field if necessary shall be unsanguined with the heart's blood of our foes upon its folds. I here inscribed 'Right shall make Might' and every honest heart speaking the truth to itself must acknowledge that our cause is right and just . . . Wherever it is planted, may it be a demarking line to the nearer approaches of those insolent . . . hordes that now threaten our very fireside."

Captain Hart then presented the guidon to the color bearer, Louis Sherfesee. Through 143 engagements the guidon led the Washington Artillery, and Sherfesee brought it home at last unsurrendered.

The reverse of this 18" (hoist) x 41" (fly) guidon is different from the obverse. On the garnet top section is embroidered a palmetto tree and a crescent in ecru. On the lower ecru section are embroidered the words RIGHT SHALL MAKE MIGHT in red 2½" letters. Three red-and-white rosettes are attached to the side of the guidon.

The guidon is in fragile and extremely faded condition.

South Carolina Relic Room & Museum, Columbia, S.C.

German Artillery
Company B, Artillery Battalion, Hampton Legion

Captain William K. Bachmann's Company of artillery went to Virginia as Company B, Artillery Battalion, Hampton Legion. After the reorganization of 1862, the battery was assigned to Frobel's Battalion, Hood's Division, and served in that capacity through the Battle of Gettysburg. In late summer of 1863, they were transferred back to South Carolina.

This flag was carried and retained at the end of the war by A.W. Jager, guidon bearer of the battery.

Battle honors are sewn to the field in separately cut-out white cotton 2" block letters. Honors on the reverse correspond to the obverse in the following manner.

This flag is 44¾" (hoist) x 43" (fly).

Confederate Museum, Charleston, S.C.

Obverse		Reverse
MANASSAS 2nd (20" long)	*corresponds to*	GETTYSBURG (17½" long)
SUFFOLK (11½")		WEST POINT (7½", 8¼")
COCKPIT POINT (11", 8½")		GAINS MILL (9½", 8")
MECHANICSVILLE (24")		FREDERICKSBURG (24")
BOONSBORO (17")		MEYERS FARM (18½")
SHARPSBURG (18")		FRAZERS FARM (20")

Ferguson's (S.C.) Artillery Company
(Beauregard's Battery)

Ferguson's (S.C.) Artillery Company was organized in Charleston and turned over to Confederate service on April 4, 1862. The company was commanded by Captain Thomas Barker Ferguson and 1st Lieutenant René T. Beauregard and was stationed at various places in the Charleston area, including James Island, Sullivan's Island, and Summerville.

In May 1863, the company was attached to General States R. Gist's brigade and traveled west, joining the Army of Tennessee. They were engaged at the siege of Jackson, Mississippi, where on July 14, 1863, Captain Ferguson was shot through the lung. He survived the wound and traveled back to South Carolina but never rejoined the battery. 1st Lieutenant Beauregard assumed command and led the battery back through Alabama and Georgia. Beauregard's Battery was engaged in the Tunnell Hill area of Missionary Ridge on November 25, 1863. After a severe fight, they were assigned rear guard to cover the army's retreat. On the night of November 26, 1863, they were ambushed outside Graysville, Georgia. They lost half their armament, a fourth of their men, and the above Charleston issue flag.

Museum of the Confederacy, Richmond, Va.

Ferguson's (S.C.) Artillery Co.
(Beauregard's Battery)

It is highly unlikely that concerned ladies of the South made this haphazardly designed guidon. It is much more likely that this is a temporary banner made to replace the company battle flag that was captured at Graysville, Georgia, on the retreat from Missionary Ridge.

Made of blue wool, the edges are unhemmed. The pole sleeve is made of duck and is 2⅛" wide. The hoist is 18" and the fly is 17½". The irregularly shaped star is made of muslin and is sewn on with a simple whipstitch. The letters are painted on in gold paint. The flag is finished only on the obverse side.

South Carolina Confederate Relic Room & Museum, Columbia, S.C.

Palmetto Artillery

During the winter of 1997-98, this flag was offered at auction by Gary Hendershott of Little Rock, Arkansas. It was described as the "Confederate flag of the famous Palmetto Artillery that fired the first shot of the Civil War." This statement seems to be an advertising ploy. There have been many arguments concerning who fired the "first shot" of the war, none of which has proven the point. Some uphold Cadet George Haynesworth as the one who deserves the honor. On January 9, 1861, he fired the first shot at the Star of the West from the Cadet battery on Morris Island. Some say Edmund Ruffin, honorary member of the Palmetto Guard, fired the first shot on April 12, 1861, touching off the two-day bombardment of Fort Sumter. No other historical details were mentioned in the advertisement.

The two units officially designated "Palmetto Artillery," the *3rd (White's) Battalion and Captain Garden's Battery*, were not organized at the time of the firing of Sumter.

Nevertheless, this is an interesting flag. It is likely of South Carolina manufacture; the ten stars are laid out in a crescent design, with the central star representing the first state to secede.

In a private collection.

Lafayette Artillery
Captain J. T. Kanapaux's Co.

This French-speaking company was organized in the early 1800s as the *Fusiliers Français*, and served as the official escort of the Marquis de Lafayette during his American visit in 1824. Around 1840, it changed its service to light artillery and became Charleston's first Light Artillery Company.

The **Lafayette Artillery** served throughout the war, participating in battles at Pocotaligo and Honey Hill, and marched north with the army at the fall of Charleston in February 1865. At Bentonville they were attached to Cleburne's old division and surrendered at Greensboro, North Carolina, on May 1, 1865.

This 34½" (hoist) x 36" (fly) Charleston Depot battle flag was not surrendered, but was concealed by the color bearer and returned to Charleston.

Confederate Museum, Charleston, S.C.

Wagner Light Artillery
Company D, 3rd (Palmetto) Battalion Light Artillery

This guidon of the **Wagner Light Artillery** is 26" (hoist) x 38" (fly). It is entirely sewn construction, all of the letters being sewn on individually, and tucked and hemmed around the edges. The "D" is of white cotton and is 4³/₈" wide. The lower letters are of red cotton and are 2⁷/₈" high. The "P," "B," "L," and "A" are 2", 2¹/₈", 1³/₄", and 2⁷/₈" wide respectively. The periods are ³/₄" square. The banner was tied to the staff by three pairs of red-twill ribbons.

The Wagner Light Artillery was mustered into service on November 14, 1861, under the command of Captain Charles E. Kanapaux. That winter they were stationed at "Camp Heyward." The following spring they were transferred to "Camp Riley near Wappoo Creek." Later stations were Holmes Farm, James Island; Minett's Bluff, James Island; St. Andrew's Parish; and Secessionville.

In July 1864, they were in St. Paul's Parish near Toogadoo Bridge. The following entry is recorded in their company muster rolls.

"On Sunday morning, 3rd July, 1864, this battery was in position at the causeway (over King's Creek) leading to Star's (?) Island. The enemy landed at White Point and advanced up the Island. About 6 o'clock a.m., the battery opened upon this advance of the enemy, and the action lasted until 11 o'clock a.m. the enemy retired during Sunday and Monday night and the Battery returned to camp on Monday, 4 July. No casualties in this company."

From September to December 1864, their camp was near Toogadoo Bridge. The company was disbanded at the fall of Charleston in February 1865.

This flag used by the Wagner Light Artillery was probably made and given to the company prior to the issue of the garnet-and-black guidons. It is a headquarters-style flag, and might have been used to mark Captain Kanapaux's headquarters while in camp.

Each company of Colonel White's 3rd (Palmetto) Battalion Light Artillery carried colors similar to that of the Wagner Light Artillery. The companies that made up the Palmetto Battalion were:

Company A	*Furman Artillery*	Capt. W.E. Earle
Company B	*Waties' Battery*	Capt. John Waties
Company C	*Culpeper Artillery*	Capt. Jas. F. Culpeper
Company D	*Wagner Artillery*	Capt. Chas. F. Kanapaux
Company E		Capt. John D. Johnson
Company F	*Chesnut Artillery*	Capt. Fredk. C. Schulz
Company G	*DePass' Battery*	Capt W.C. DePass
Company H		Capt. Thos. A. Holtzclaw
Company I		Capt. J. R. Bowden
Company K		Capt. Sam'l M. Richardson

Both flags of the Wagner Light Artillery are in the collection of the South Carolina Confederate Relic Room & Museum, Columbia, S.C.

Chesnut Light Artillery
Company F, 3rd (Palmetto) Battalion Light Artillery

The **Chesnut Light Artillery,** also known as Shultz's Battery, was organized in late 1861. Throughout their history, they served in the Charleston area, seeing action on and around James Island, Legareville, and the Stono River.

The reverse of the flag of the **Chesnut Light Artillery** is readable. The stitches holding the letters on the opposite side are actually visible in the reverse. It was held to the staff by three pairs of red-twill ribbons.

Chicago Historical Society, Chicago, Ill.

The **Chesnut Artillery** was the most photographed of South Carolina's artillery units. The reason could be an incident that occurred on January 29, 1863. During the fall of 1862, a Federal gunboat, the U.S.S. *Isaac P. Smith,* was on duty patrolling the Stono River south of Charleston. Never a danger or threat to Confederate forces, it nevertheless was a nuisance. With a confidence bordering on arrogance, the officers of the ship often came ashore for picnics and to practice target shooting with their small arms. On January 28, 1863, a trap was laid at the request of General P.G.T. Beauregard. Heavy and light artillery were positioned along the banks of the river. The gunboat would be allowed to sail as far up the river as she chose, but on her return downstream she would find herself running a gauntlet of fire. On the morning of January 29, the trap was sprung. As the gunboat fled past Grimball's Plantation, the howitzer section of the Chesnut Artillery opened fire. Escaping steam billowed from the ship's boilers. She had been struck three times. A white flag from the mast signaled the end of the fight. It is said to be the only instance in the history of the war where a regular warship surrendered to soldiers manning field batteries.

Marion Light Artillery
Capt. Edward L. Parker's Company

The **Marion Artillery** was organized on June 6, 1862. During the summer of that year, the battery was stationed at Simmons Bluff, near Charleston. Through the winter, they were stationed at "Camp Echo," three miles from the river. On May 10, 1863, one section, under Lt. Strohicker, moved to James Island to participate in an attack on Seabrooks Island. Company returns say that the "Expedition failed through treachery in the crews of torpedo boats." The section returned on June 14, and two days later the battery moved into its summer quarters about one mile east of their former camp.

Washington Light Infantry, Charleston, S.C.

Through the summer of 1863, they manned the east lines of James Island. On July 10, the Napoleon section, under Lt. Murdoch, went to Wiltown Bluff and engaged a gunboat, which was fired and burned to the water's edge. On July 15, the battery was ordered to Secessionville to support advanced skirmishers (25th Regiment Infantry), fought a Union battery of rifle guns, and was shelled by gunboats in Folly River. They wintered at Church Flats and participated in an attack on gunboats at Legareville.

The company guidon alludes to one of South Carolina's greatest heroes, partisan ranger Francis Marion, the Swamp Fox of the Revolution.

Washington Artillery
Capt. George H. Walter's Battery

The **Washington Artillery Company** of Charleston was an established militia company long before the War Between the States, and was among the first troops to report for duty after the Ordinance of Secession was signed. Capt. George H. Walter was commander.

After the bombardment of Fort Sumter, to accommodate men eager to serve outside the state, the Washington Artillery split into two separate batteries. One company would win fame in Virginia as *Hart's Battery, Hampton's Horse Artillery;* the other, *Walter's Light Battery,* remained in South Carolina. They served in various roles of picket and guard duty around the Charleston area and were stationed at Adams Run and John's Island. They remained in the Charleston area until the city was evacuated in February 1865. At their surrender in North Carolina, they were attached to Major Basil C. Manly's Artillery Battalion of Cheatham's Corps.

Confederate Museum, Charleston, S.C.

Naval Ensign

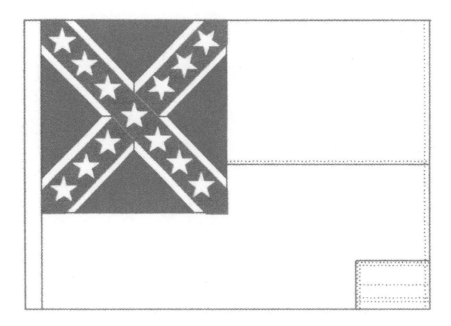

A **Naval Ensign** is a National flag that is flown from the mast of a ship. It is normally flown from the stern-most mast of a sailing ship. Although there were no regulations for it, most likely the first naval ensign was patterned after the 1st National Flag.

On May 26, 1863, Secretary of the Navy Stephen R. Mallory adopted regulations for the navy flags that brought the navy flag regulations in line with the government regulations of May 1, 1863, establishing the 2nd National flag as the official ensign. According to Naval regulations its width was to be two-thirds its length.

The above flag is actually a *storm ensign,* made with smaller measurements to be used in inclement weather. It is 36" (hoist) x 50" (fly), with a 24"-square canton. It was carried by the *C.S.S. Shenandoah* on its famous cruise of October 19, 1864 to November 6, 1865.

This flag was presented to the Washington Light Infantry by Lieutenant Thomas Grimball.

Washington Light Infantry, Charleston, S.C.

Naval Commission Pennant

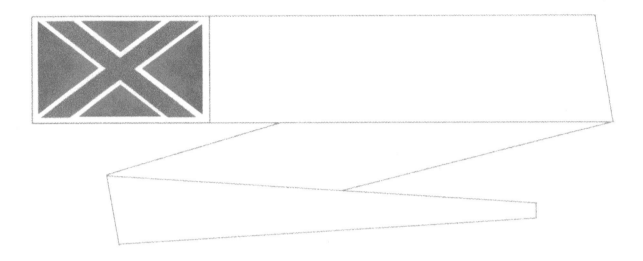

During the War Between the States, ships commonly flew three types of flags: the **Ensign,** the **Jack,** and the **Commission Pennant.** Each flag had a designated location on the ship and served a particular purpose.

Commission pennants were flown from the top of the highest mast on a ship. On a sailing vessel, this would be the mainmast. Naval commission pennants indicate the nationality of a ship and show that the ship is commissioned in the service of that nation. There were no published regulations for the Confederate Navy's pennant before 1863. The first Confederate commission pennant had a single row of seven stars on a blue field and a long trailing body composed of three stripes, red/white/red, terminating in a swallowtail tip.

A new regulation of 1863 provided for a new commission pennant. The length was unusually long: 72 times the width at the head, tapering to a point. The new pennant had thirteen stars and a long trailing solid white body.

There were many pennants, known as variant pennants, that did not meet regulations. The one above is such a pennant.

Confederate Museum, Charleston, S.C.

Naval Jack

The **Jack** is flown only on a ship of war when in port, from the jack staff at the bow of the ship. It designates a ship's nationality.

On May 26, 1863, in conjunction with the adoption of a new national flag, the secretary of the navy issued regulations calling for new flags for his department.

"THE JACK. To be the same as the union for the Ensign, except that its length shall be one and a half times its width." The ensign in this case was the 2nd National Flag. By taking the "union" and giving it a 2:3 ratio, the new naval jack took on the look of Johnston's rectangular Battle Flag of the Army of Tennessee.

Prior to the above directive, the ship's Jack was taken from the canton of the 1st National flag and was a rectangular blue flag with a circle of stars in the center.

The Jack shown above, though in nonconformance to Naval regulations, was most likely used after 1863. It is 22¼" (hoist) x 30½" (fly). It is made of red flannel and has a ⁵⁄₁₆" white border.

South Carolina Confederate Relic Room & Museum, Columbia, S.C.

Dimensions of the Battle Flags

In the table below, the dimensions are represented by the following code:

a: hoist	f: star diameter
b: fly	g: center to 1st star
c: bar width	h: center to 2nd star
d: fimbriation	i: center to 3rd star
e: border width	

Flag	a	b	c	d	e	f	g	h	i
Infantry									
2nd Regt.	48	48¼	5¼	½	2	3¼	6½	13	19
3rd Regt.	47	48½	4¼	½	2	3½	6	12	18½
Palmetto S.S.[2]	48½	48	5	½	1⅞	3⅜	6	12	18
6th Regt.	46	48			2				
7th Regt.	49	50½	5⅛	½	2	4½	8-8½	15½	23-24
7th Bn.	48	48	8½	1¼	2¾	3¾	8	16	24
8th Regt.	46	46	5¼	½	1¾	3¼	6¼	12½	19
10th Regt.	35	51	6½	2	n/a	4			
11th Regt.	44¾	45½	8	¾	2¼	4¼	7¾	15½	24
12th Regt.	31½	34							
13th Regt.	44	44	5½	½	1¾	3½	6	12	18
14th Regt.	34	48	4⅜	¼	n/a	4⅜	7-8	14-17	24-26
15th Regt.	40	46	5	½	2	3¼			
16th Regt.	48	47	8¼	⅞	2¼	4	8-8½	16½	23-24
Shpsbg. Flg.	52½	56			1½				
21st Regt.[2]	46½	47	5	½	1½	3⅝	5½	11½	17½
21st Regt.[3]	46	48¾	8¼	1	1¾	4	8	16	24
Wallace's	45	45	7	1¼	1¾	4¼			
24th Regt.	44	47	7¾	¾	2¾	3¼			
25th Regt.	45½	48	8	1	2¼	4¼	8	16	24
26th Regt.	41	41			2				
27th Regt.	45⅞	45¼	7¾	¾	2½	4¼	7½	15½	23

Artillery

Bachmann's	$44^3/_4$	43	$4^1/_2$	$^1/_2$	2	$3^1/_2$	6	12	18
Charles'	34	34	5	$^7/_8$	2	$3^1/_4$	$5^1/_2$	11	$16^1/_2$
Ferguson's	34	34	$5^1/_2$	1	$2^1/_2$	$3^1/_4$	$5^1/_2$	11	$16^1/_2$
Lafayette	$34^1/_2$	36	5	$^3/_4$	2	$3^1/_8$	$5^1/_2$	$10^3/_4$	16
Washington	35	36	$4^3/_4$	1	$2^1/_4$	3	$5^1/_2$	11	$16^1/_2$
3rd Regt.									
Heavy	45	47	8	1	2	$3^3/_4$	8	16	24

Cavalry

5th Regt.[1]									
5th Regt.[2]	$50^1/_2$	$50^1/_2$	$6^1/_2$	$^5/_8$	$1^7/_8$	$5^1/_2$	8	16	24

Bibliography

Baldwin, James J., III, *A Biography of the Struck Eagle, Brigadier-General Micah Jenkins: A History of the Fifth South Carolina Volunteers and the Palmetto Sharpshooters.* Shippensburg, PA: Burd Street Press, 1996.

Batson, Mann, *The Colors of the Sixteenth South Carolina.* http://members.theglobe.com/gbatsonsmb/franklin8.html.

Batson, Mann, *The Return of the Flags.* http://members.theglobe.com/batsonsmb/after2.html.

Beckman, David, *Confederate Flags, Unfurled!* http://www.geocities.com/CapitolHill/3416/unfurled.html.

Bragg, C.L., *Confederate Veteran,* article "Captain Moses Benbow Humphrey: Cadet Ranger from the Citadel," Volume 4, 1997.

Burton, E. Milby, *The Siege of Charleston,* 1861-1865. Columbia: University of South Carolina Press, 1970.

Capers, Ellison, *Confederate Military History: South Carolina.* Atlanta: Confederate Publishing Co., 1899.

Chapman, John A., *History of Edgefield County from the Earliest Settlements to 1897.* Greenville: Southern Historical Press, Inc. 1976 (reprint from the 1897 original).

Coker, James Lide, *History of Company G, Ninth S.C. Regiment, Infantry, S.C. Army and of Company E, Sixth S.C. Regiment, Infantry, S.C. Army.* Greenwood: Attic Press, Inc., 1979 (reprint from original).

Crute, Joseph H., Jr., *Emblems of Southern Valor: The Battle Flags of the Confederacy.* Louisville: Harmony House, 1990.

Crute, Joseph H., *Units of the Confederate States Army.* Midlothian, VA: Derwent Books, 1987.

Edwards, W.H., Capt., *A Condensed History of the Seventeenth Regiment, S.C.V., C.S.A.* Originally completed by Capt. Edwards in 1906 and printed by Miss Helen G. McMaster in January of 1908; in the collection of the S.C. State Archives.

Field, Ron, *South Carolina Volunteers in the Civil War*. Gloucestershire: Design Folio
   1st South Carolina Volunteers (Gregg's), 1991.
   4th South Carolina Volunteers (Sloan's), 1992.
   5th South Carolina Volunteers (Jenkins'), 1997.
   7th South Carolina Volunteers (Bacon's), 1993.
   The Hampton Legion, Part 1: Regimental History, 1994.
   The Hampton Legion, Part II: Company Histories, 1995.

Gragg, Rod, *The Illustrated Confederate Reader*. New York: Harper & Row, 1989; article "Another Hero Takes the Falling Standard," pp. 122-23.

Grissom, Michael A., *Southern by the Grace of God*. Gretna: Pelican Publishing Co., 1990.

Izlar, William Valmore, *Edisto Rifles*. Columbia: The State Co., 1914.

Jones, Eugene W., Jr., *Enlisted for the War: The Struggles of the Gallant 24th Regiment, South Carolina Volunteers, Infantry, 1861-1865*. Highstown, NJ: Longstreet House, 1997.

Katcher, Scollins, Embleton, *Flags of the American Civil War 1:* Confederate, Men-at-Arms Series, No. 252. London: Osprey Publishing, Ltd., 1992.

Madaus, Howard Michael, *The Battle Flags of the Confederate Army* of *Tennessee*. Milwaukee: Milwaukee Public Museum, 1976.

Reid, J.W., *History of the Fourth Regiment S.C. Volunteers from the Commencement of the War until Lee's Surrender*. Dayton: Morningside Book Shop, 1975 (reprint of 1891 edition).

Rose, Rebecca Ansel, *Colours of the Gray: An Illustrated Index of Wartime Flags From the Museum of the Confederacy's Collection*. Richmond: 1998.

Ruth, David R., *The Authentication of the Palmetto Flag Owned and Carried by John Styles Bird During His Service With the Palmetto Guard*. Fort Sumter National Monument, July 1983.

Sifakis, Stewart, *Compendium of the Confederate Armies: South Carolina and Georgia*. New York: Facts-on-File, 1995.

South Carolina Division United Daughters of the Confederacy, *Recollections and Reminiscences 1861-1865*. United Daughters of the Confederacy.
   Vol. III, p. 258-59, *Hampton Legion*.
   Vol. III, p. 291-95, *The Johnson Rifles*.
   Vol. III, p. 305-7, *The Flag of the Pee Dee Light Artillery*.

Vol. III, p. 412, *The Flag of the Pea Ridge Volunteers.*
Vol. V, p. 95, *The Saluda Guards Flag.*
Vol. V, p. 96, *A State Flag.*
Vol. V, p. 97, *Governor's Guards Flag.*

Topper, Celeste; Topper, David, *Civil War Relics from South Carolina.* Fairfax, SC: 1988.

U.S. Government, *The Flags of the Confederate Armies Returned to the Men Who Bore Them by the United States Government.* 1905.

Walker, C.I., *10th Regiment S.C. Volunteers, Confederate States Army, Rolls and Sketch.* Charleston: Walker, Evans & Cogswell, 1881.

Woodhead, Henry, ed., *Echoes of Glory: Arms and Equipment of the Confederacy.* New York: Time-Life, 1991.

Flags Not Illustrated
S.C. Confederate Relic Room

1. Stainless Banner
2. 2ⁿᵈ Confederate National
3. Castle Pinckney

   The above three flags are of the 2ⁿᵈ National type.
4. Hartley Flag
5. Cedar Creek Rifles Flag

   This flag is in shreds. The blue field is evident and some gold fringe remains, but the seal is unrecognizable.
6. Catawba Rangers Flag

   A beautiful blue flag with full fringe. The obverse shows a palmetto tree, brown trunk, green fronds, on a grassy island. White banner arches over. White banner arches under. Tree surrounded by open-topped garland of white and red flowers. The reverse has a red 5-pointed star in the center. To the left of the star is "S." in gold. To the right is a "C." in gold. Below star is a hand with index finger pointed skyward. Gold garland of lilies. White banner over. White banner under.
7. Lone Star Flag
8. First Confederate National
9. Darlington Guards Flag
10. Secession Guards Flag
11. Pacolet Volunteers, 13ᵗʰ Regt., Co. K
12. 15ᵗʰ Regt., Co. A

    This is a very badly damaged flag. The entire center, possibly the seal, is gone. No discernible markings. It is faded and shredded. However, the fringe is intact on three sides.
13. Beauregard Lt. Inf., 25ᵗʰ Regt., Co. E

Charleston Museum

1. Brooks Artillery
2. 1ˢᵗ National

   This large (80" x 133") flag has ties to the 7ᵗʰ S.C. Infantry Regiment. Unusual, perhaps post-war, in that it has metal grommets.

S.C. State Museum

1. S.C. Confederate Unit Flag
   Too fragile to unroll.
2. Mercer Guards, 17th Regt., S.C.M.
   Too fragile to unroll.

Confederate Museum

1. 3rd National, Petersburg flag
2. Ft. Sumter 2nd National
3. 2nd National
   Unmarked, good condition.
4. S.C. Flag (Dum Spiro Spero)

Chicago Historical Society

1. Saluda Sentinels
2. Charleston Rifles

National Museum of the Civil War Soldier at Pamplin Park

1. 27th S.C. Regiment
   Standard unmarked Charleston Depot flag.

Union County Historical Society

1. Tiger River Volunteers

Appreciation

Vexillologists of the War Between the States period owe an inestimable debt to Howard Michael Madaus. His pioneering efforts in researching the flags of the 1860s have left a wealth of knowledge that has been invaluable in producing this work.

Many thanks to James J. Baldwin III, *author and historian, Greenville, S.C.;* John Bigham, *S.C. Confederate Relic Room & Museum, Columbia, S.C.;* Randy Burbage, *descendant, James Island, S.C.;* George "Buck" Carpenter, *descendant, Trenton, S.C.;* Dr. Allan Charles, *Union County Historical Museum, Union, S.C.;* Donald Christopoulo, *descendant, New Ellenton, S.C.;* Robert & Frances Freeman, *Charleston, S.C.;* James Gabel, *descendant, Rapid City, S.D.;* John A. Guy, III, Capt., *Washington Light Infantry, Charleston, S.C.;* Fritz Hamer, *S.C. State Museum, Columbia, S.C.;* Richard Hatcher, III, *Fort Sumter NM, Charleston, S.C.;* Jan Hiester, *The Charleston Museum, Charleston, S.C.;* Paul Rush Mitchell, *Thomasville, N.C.;* Bonnie Moffat, *S.C. Confederate Relic Room & Museum, Columbia, S.C.;* Katherine Richardson, *Sumter County Museum, Sumter, S.C.;* Gary Roberts, *Chester County Historical Society, Chester, S.C.;* Rebecca A. Rose, *Curator of the Flag Collection, Museum of the Confederacy, Richmond, Va.;* Elizabeth K. Shoemaker, *Special Collections, Emory Univ., Atlanta, Ga.;* Helen Bowen Tedards, *Greenville, S.C.;* Rosalind Tedards, *Greenville, S.C.;* Ron Weaver, *Emmaus, Pa.;* and June Murray Wells, *Confederate Museum, Charleston, S.C.*

Love and appreciation to my wife, Donna, for uncountable acts of support that allowed me to finish this work; for hours of proofreading, corrections, and suggestions; for handling organizational contacts through letters and phone; and for loving patience with me as I pursued this dream.

Used With Permission

6. Photo: *Sovereignty Flag,* Chester County Historical Society, Chester, S.C.

25. Painting: *The Charge at Trevilian Station,* Mort Kunstler, Oyster Bay, N.Y.

65. Painting: *The 10th S.C. Regiment,* Rick Reeves, Tampa, Fla.

67. Painting: *Iron Courage, Southern Chivalry,* Henry Kidd, Colonial Heights, Va.

104. Photo: *Chesnut Light Artillery,* Valentine Museum, Richmond, Va.

104. Photo: *F Company Flag,* Chicago Historical Society, Chicago, Ill.

All other photographs by author.